W9-AVC-388

hamlyn

small garden solutions

Richard Bird

CONTENTS

Publishing Director: Alison Goff
Creative Director: Keith Martin
Executive Editor: Julian Brown
Editor: Karen O'Grady
Executive Art Editor: Mark Winwood
Design: Birgit Eggers
Picture Research: Wendy Gay
Production: Joanna Walker
Special Photography: Mark Winwood
Illustration: Pond & Giles

First published in Great Britain in 2000
by Hamlyn, an imprint of
Octopus Publishing Group Limited
2–4 Heron Quays, London, E14 4JP

Copyright © 2000 Octopus Publishing Group
Limited

ISBN 0 600 596710

A catalogue record for this book is available
from the British Library

Produced by Toppan
Printed in China

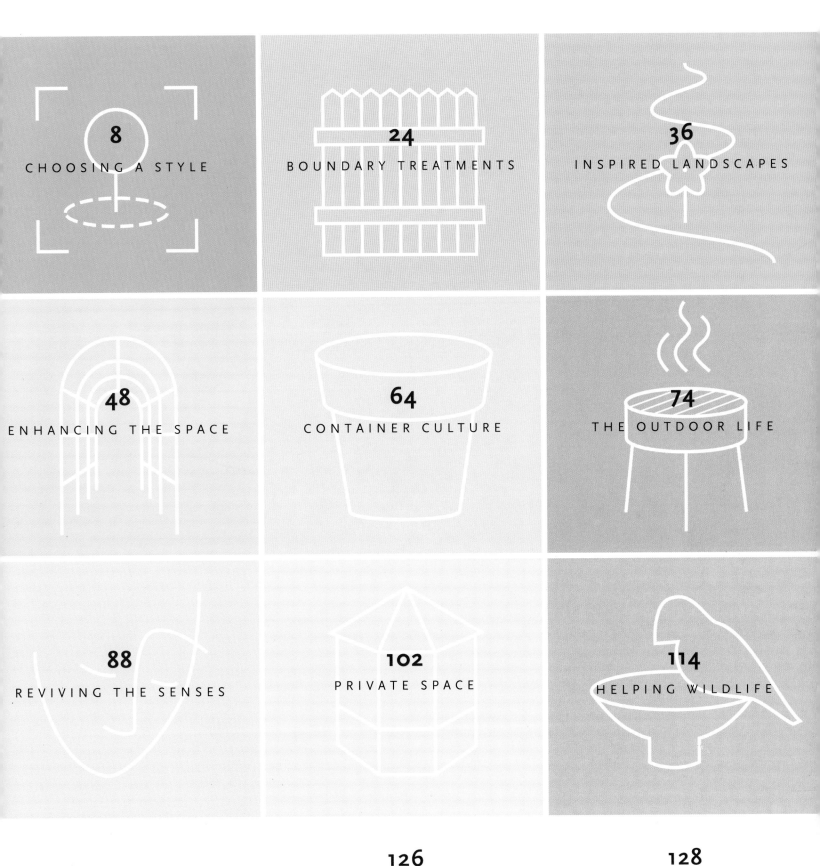

INTRODUCTION

PLANNING   CARRYING OUT YOUR PLANS   ENJOYMENT

How small is a small garden? As small or as big as you like. You can create a small garden on a roof or a miniature one on a balcony. On the other hand, a large garden of two acres can be subdivided into a number of small gardens, each with its own character. Most modern gardens, however, are small, often 10 x 10m (30 x 30ft) or less. The equivalent houses built forty or fifty years ago would have had much larger gardens, often 30m (100ft) long. This book caters for all of those gardens. The ideas can be scaled up or down to fit the space available, although, obviously, the number of different ideas that can be incorporated into any one plot will vary. In a long, narrow garden several different types of area can be included, perhaps separated from each other by screens; in a small, compact garden it will be necessary to concentrate on creating a single picture with just on or two ideas.

There are three distinct phases to creating or making over a garden or outside space, each of them pleasurable in a different way. The first phase is the planning: the process of deciding what you want and how you are going to achieve it. The second stage is carrying out your plans. Even if you do not do all the work yourself, there is still the excitement of anticipation and watching the new garden begin to take shape. The third and, for most people, the most important aspect is the enjoyment that comes from being in and using the garden.

This last aspect, the enjoyment of your garden, is entirely up to you, and no one can help you, but we can help with the other two elements of the process, which establish the framework for that pleasure and create the environment in which that pleasure can be achieved. In this book we set out to give you ideas: ideas about what you can do with your space and how to adapt it to your own tastes and lifestyle. We also aim to help you bring some of these ideas into reality with practical advice.

For many people planning a garden is the most difficult task of all: 'Where do I start?' There is little point in aimlessly doodling on a piece of paper. The first thing is to try to define exactly what you want from your garden. Write down a list of everything you want to do in the garden. You might simply want to grow plants because you are a keen gardener; you might want a lawn for the children to play on; you might want flowerbeds for cut flowers; you might want somewhere to grow your own vegetables; you might want a barbecue area so that you can entertain your friends; you might want nothing more than a peaceful, quiet place where you can relax at weekends and on warm summer evenings. Jot down everything you can think of at this stage – nothing is too fanciful, and there might just be a way to make it work.

It is quite likely that this list will be far too long for a small garden, or it may be too time or money consuming. These factors – space, time and money – have now to be reconciled with what you would like to do. Some things may well have to have to go. Having a swimming pool, for example, might be desirable, but lack of space or lack of funds, or both, might rule it out right from the start. Other things, even with a great deal of thought may be irreconcilable. For example, children playing ball games and large flowerbeds are unlikely to coexist in a small garden, and football and greenhouses may be another apparently incompatible combination. Stop and think for a minutes, however: perhaps if there were a screen or trellis in front of the greenhouse it might just work.

Think of the future as well as the present. The children will not be children for ever. Plant a tree by the lawn on which they tear around playing football, and by the time they move on to other pursuits it will be big enough for you to relax in its shade, using the lawn for quite a different purpose. What is a now child's sandpit may, one day, be converted into a pond. A sandpit should be positioned so that you can keep an eye on the children from the patio or the kitchen window; later on the pond will be a focal point in the garden. Both features require the same kind of position, but for different reasons, and, with a little thought, the same construction.

Once you have narrowed down your ideas to practical proportions, draw up a plan. Keep trying different ideas until you arrive at the optimum solution. It may be that you can get a more elements in than you had originally thought. Perhaps you suddenly find a niche for a barbecue that you thought you would have to sacrifice. On the other hand, try as you may, you may have to forgo a shed or a border to get it to fit. Try to visualize the space when it is laid out. Avoid cramming too many things in. They may look fine on the plan, but in the real world your garden might begin to look like a junk room.

Once you have decided what you want to do and where you will do it, it is time to turn your plans into reality. You may like to get somebody in to do it. This costs money and you will have to give clear instructions of what you want. The advantages are that it is comparatively quick and it saves you work. On the other hand, there is a great deal of enjoyment to be derived from carrying out the work yourself. Not only does it save a lot of money, but you can adapt things as you go along and you need not commit yourself to doing all the work at once.

On the pages that follow are plenty of ideas to get you started on transforming your garden. Look at the pictures, read the text and then sit down with that pencil and paper and start planning.

CHOOSING A STYLE

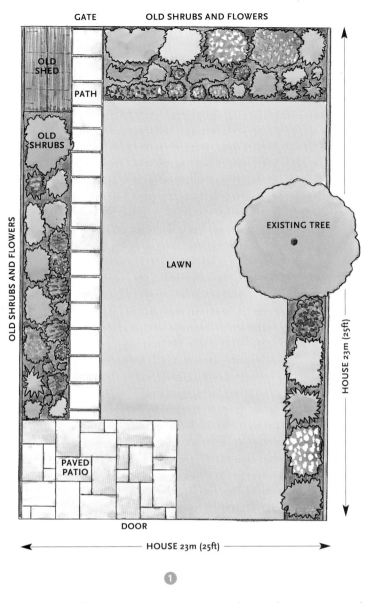

GATE   OLD SHRUBS AND FLOWERS

OLD SHED

PATH

OLD SHRUBS

OLD SHRUBS AND FLOWERS

EXISTING TREE

LAWN

HOUSE 23m (25ft)

PAVED PATIO

DOOR

HOUSE 23m (25ft)

❶

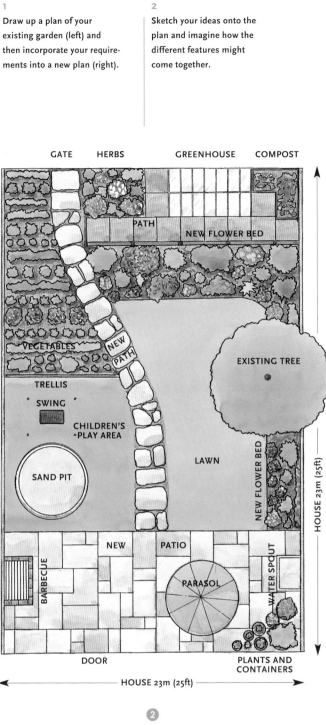

1 Draw up a plan of your existing garden (left) and then incorporate your requirements into a new plan (right).

2 Sketch your ideas onto the plan and imagine how the different features might come together.

GATE   HERBS   GREENHOUSE   COMPOST

PATH   NEW FLOWER BED

VEGETABLES   NEW PATH

EXISTING TREE

TRELLIS

SWING

CHILDREN'S PLAY AREA

SAND PIT

LAWN

NEW FLOWER BED

HOUSE 23m (25ft)

BARBECUE   NEW   PATIO

PARASOL

WATER SPOUT

DOOR   PLANTS AND CONTAINERS

HOUSE 23m (25ft)

❷

You do not have be a garden designer to choose the way your garden looks. After all, most of us manage to decorate the inside of our homes to our own satisfaction, so why should we not be capable of doing the same outside? Anyway, it's fun.

The first thing to do when laying out a garden is to decide what style you want. There are styles to suit everybody and that will be able to reflect your tastes and your lifestyle. There are no rules about what you should like: choosing a garden style is an entirely personal matter. If you have a busy, regimented working life, an informal, relaxed style of garden may be to your liking to provide a contrast. On the other hand, you may be formal both on and off duty and always prefer things to be neat and tidy, in which case the clear-cut lines of a formal garden may be your choice.

Remember that you have to live with the garden, so do not choose a style that you will be unable to keep up nor one that conflicts with your lifestyle. Children and precise formal gardens do not mix, for example,so wait until the children have left home.There are plenty of variations within each style from which you can chose. Each formal garden, for example, follows roughly the same principles, but each has a different scale, shape, pattern and colour. If all this sounds daunting there is no need to worry; some of the best gardeners have never had any training in aesthetics or design; instead, they work entirely by eye.

PREPARING A BASIC GARDEN PLAN

The first step in drawing up a plan is to work out exactly what you want to do in the garden. Draw up a list of requirements. Next measure out the garden and draw a plan showing existing features and their position relative to each other. It is easiest to follow if this is on squared paper. Once this is done, make several copies of this basic plan and then draw in, roughly at first, the positions of the various areas and items that you want. Once satisfied that everything is in the right place and will fit in, draw out the definitive copy with everything drawn to scale.

PLANTS FOR BALANCE AND SYMMETRY

Buxus sempervirens (common box)
Cordyline australis
   (New Zealand cabbage palm)
Juniperus scopulorum 'Skyrocket'
Laurus nobilis (sweetbay)
Lavandula angustifolia (lavender)
Miscanthus sinensis
Rosa (rose: standard bushes)
Santolina pinnata subsp. *neapolitana*
Taxus baccata (yew)
Yucca gloriosa (Spanish dagger)

THE FORMAL GARDEN

Many people like to have total control over their lives, and the use of formal designs within and outside the house is one way of achieving this aim. The clean-cut, almost severe, lines of such designs are not just a symbol of control, however, for there is also great pleasure to be had from the elegance of such designs.

One of the keys to a formal design is simplicity. All fussiness is removed, and restraint is imposed. The lines and shapes are usually simple, consisting of straight lines and regular curves. Out go tortuously curved borders stuffed with flowers. In come squares, rectangles, circles and ellipses. Triangles and stars, unless they are within a design, are usually avoided because the points of such geometric features are usually too sharp for planting.

Symmetry is another key to formality. Patterns should be regular, and plantings should be balanced from one side of the bed to another. The regular planting of trees or shrubs or the positioning of containers along a path or around a bed creates a pleasing rhythm that adds to the formality.

Not everything need needs to be balanced, of course. Often a single plant or container as a focal point works extremely well. These need not be symmetrical to the design. A clump of grass and a group of rocks, for example, could be placed to one side of a space, rather than being positioned in the very centre.

KEY ELEMENTS

The basis of the design is provided by gravel or regularly paved areas. Within this framework are various structures and beds, all preferably with a regular outline. Ponds are not wild, natural ones, but are regularly shaped, often lined with concrete and with a fountain or spout. Containers with a single plant, often a clipped tree or shrub, are a popular way of displaying plants. Plants are also often contained within a formal parterre or knot garden. These consist of low, clipped hedges of box. Instead of being filled with plants, the areas contained by these hedges can either be left empty or filled with brightly coloured gravel.

Planting should be restrained and simple. Use single plants, perhaps in pots stood at strategic positions. Avoid mixing too many colours and anything that needs a great deal of maintenance. Many formal gardens rely almost entirely on foliage. Some people like to grow only trees and shrubs, partly because of their green foliage, but also because the foliage can be controlled by clipping.

MARKING OUT CIRCLES ON THE GROUND

Place a peg where the center of the circle is to be. Attach a piece of string to this and tie a sharp stick at half the diameter of the circle. Walk round the peg, keeping the string taut and scribing a mark on the ground, defining the circle. Alternatively, if the ground is hard, fill a bottle with dry sand and tie this to a string. Walk round, keeping the string taut and trickling the sand out of the bottle as you go so that it leaves a clear mark on the ground. Dig out the circle.

1
Mark out a circular bed by scoring a line with a stick on a piece of string attached to a central peg.

2
Then remove the turf from within the circle and dig it, adding plenty of well-rotted organic material.

PLANTS FOR COMFORTABLE INFORMALITY

PERENNIALS

Alchemilla mollis (lady's mantle)
Aster x frikartii
Centranthus ruber (red valerian)
Geranium macrorrhizum
Geranium pratense (meadow cranesbill)
Helleborus orientalis (Lenten rose)
Leucanthemum x superbum (shasta daisy)
Penstemon 'Andenken an Friedrich Hahn'
Persicaria affinis
Primula Polyanthus Group

SHRUBS AND TREES

Cotoneaster microphyllus
Helianthemum nummularium (rock rose)
Hypericum x inodorum 'Elstead'
Potentilla fruticosa
Pyrus salicifolia 'Pendula'
Rosa (rose: shrub and floribunda/
   hybrid tea)
Salvia officinalis (sage)
Sorbus hupehensis (Hubei rowan)
Spiraea 'Arguta' (bridal wreath)
Thymus serpyllum (creeping thyme)

COMFORTABLE INFORMALITY

Although they admire and may even hanker after a neat, formal garden, where everything is in its place, most gardeners feel more comfortable with an informal style – a garden where a football or watering can left lying around will not look out of place, a garden where a weed might just be acceptable.

Comfortable informality has its origins in the cottage garden, where vegetables and flowers were often intermixed and plants were planted not by some great complex design, but simply because there was a gap to fill. Colours were often jumbled up, with very little thought given to the overall effect – the end result was usually a riot of colour. Bright colours, especially annuals, often play a leading role in this type of garden, but there is no reason why softer, more restrained colours should not be used in the same way. This style of gardening still exists, and it has a lot to recommend it: there is no more lying awake at night wondering what plant to plant with which; you just put them in where there is a space and create a cheerful mixture of a wide variety of plants. And why not?

Not everyone feels comfortable with such anarchy. Many people prefer to take a much more controlled approach, although still outside the straightjacket imposed by a formal garden. Colours in borders can be grouped so that there is some form of harmony. Borders of single colours can be used – white or pastel colours for a peaceful setting, and red or the hot colours for more excitement. Planting can be precise rather than random, but the overall effect is one of relaxed control. Of course, flowering plants need not predominate, and the informality may come from foliage plants, including mounds of shrubs.

An informal style can sometimes mean that every detail, down to the last blade of grass, is planned, but this is not the method used by most garedeners. It usually means adopting a much more flexible approach to designing. It is, for example, a great deal easier to accommodate plants that are already in the garden. You do not have to grub everything out and start again, and shrubs, trees, existing lawns and paths can all be re-used and do not have to be moved to fit into the new scheme.

MIXING IT

An informal garden makes it possible to blend various activities together. The garden is likely to have a lived-in feeling about it and to be something that is not so much for show as to be used and enjoyed. A barbecue or child's play area will, for example, sit happily alongside decorative borders. Vegetable plots will mix with flowers and not need their own well-defined areas. Although such a layout may at first glance seem completely casual, it does actually require careful preliminary planning to make sure that the garden does not end up looking as if it was just thrown together.

An informal garden is a much more suitable environment for young children. A tangle of shrubs makes an ideal 'camp' and hiding place. No matter how much they are nagged, they will always leave playthings lying around and send balls crashing through the undergrowth, leaving temporary gaps. If the garden is likely to be used for ball games, beds with straight sides may prove to be more suitable than curved ones. A well-manicured lawn and active children do not suit each other. The practical solution is to select a tough grass, which will look far less formal but will stand up to running and cycling much better.

BORDER AND PATIO SHAPES

The shapes of the borders and patio and the lie of the paths can be anything that takes your fancy. Some are more pleasing aesthetically than others, but if a clumsily shaped patio fits the available space and feels comfortable, so be it. In general, curved beds look more appealing than those with straight edges, but it is best to avoid too extreme curves and awkward angles, which are difficult to plant successfully and hard to edge or mow up to.

When you are laying out designs for borders and patios on the ground, use a hosepipe to work out the curves. A ball of string can also be used, but it does not show up as well, and ideally you need to be able to view the proposed outlines from a distance.

GRASSES FOR THE MODERN LOOK

Calamagrostis 'Karl Foerster'

Festuca glauca

Helictotrichon sempervirens
   (blue oat grass)

Imperata cylindrica 'Rubra'
   ('Red Baron')

Melica ciliata

Milium effusum 'Aureum'
   (Bowles' golden grass)

Miscanthus sinensis 'Morning Light'

Miscanthus sinensis 'Strictus'

Molinia caerulea subsp. *arundinacea*
   'Transparent'

Pennisetum villosum (feathertop)

THE MODERN LOOK

Some people are more conscious of trends and fashions than others, and just as the inside of the house reflects this, so the garden follows suit. Gardens are generally a longer-term prospect, simply because things have to grow, but they still lend themselves to this approach.

There have always been gardens that followed the style of the day. In the past it was necessary to employ the fashionable designer to lay out your garden, but now modern styles and trends, still often designer led, are illustrated in a wide range of magazines for anyone to copy. Flicking through gardening periodicals, especially the more trendy ones, weekend supplements and fashion magazines will provide a wealth of ideas, which can be adapted to meet your own tastes and requirements.

MATERIAL CONSIDERATIONS

The materials, especially of containers, play an important role in such a garden. An earthy look, with terracotta playing a leading role, was once considered the height of fashion. Then the pots were painted. Later still, other materials took over. Galvanized containers, buckets and watering cans have played their part, and now one of the latest trends is for stainless steel.

All these materials have been in vogue at various times, and there is no reason why they should not still be used as long as you do not mind being branded *passé* by more trendy neighbours. Terracotta, for example, although it has had its high days, is a timeless material for the garden and for most gardeners will never go out of fashion.

FASHIONABLE PLANTS

As with materials, so with plants: some are more fashionable than others. In recent years, for example, there has been a resurgence of interest in grasses, which are ideal for small gardens as they can be used in so many different ways. They can look elegant and smart or tousled and unkempt. They can be grown as specimen plants or as a tangled mass. Bamboos are used in similar ways.

Brightly coloured plants, especially exotic ones such as cannas, are becoming more fashionable, and brightly coloured annuals are gradually becoming more acceptable.

PLANTING IN STYLE

The design and style of planting can also be dictated by trends and fashions. The Victorians loved elaborate bedding schemes, which involved planting out large numbers of specially raised plants in intricate schemes, but one of the more fashionable styles of the moment involves natural planting. This is the growing together of plants that would naturally associate and prosper together in the wild and doing so in a way that emulates their appearance in the wild, so there are plenty of grasses as well as more colourful plants all mixed together as you would find them in a meadow or on a roadside verge. Doubtless there will soon be a reaction against this, and the lost art of formal bedding will return.

ARTEFACTS

Another trend in modern gardens is to treat the space as an outside room and reduce the amount of actual garden. The space is paved in stone or brick and any visual interest is generated by objects of one sort or another, rather than high-maintenance, time-consuming plants. Climbers and vegetation on walls and fences are replaced by mosaics or *trompe-l'oeil*. Shrubs and trees are displaced by sculpture and *objets trouvés*, and no lawn maintenance is required because all the grass has been exchanged for hard surfacing. As well as presenting a completely different environment, all these changes also represent a major change in garden maintenance: it no longer exists.

The garden is reduced to its bare essentials. It has become a minimal, low-maintenance space. It has become a garden for those who hate or have no time for gardening, but still want an attractive space in which to relax.

PLANTS TO SPECIALIZE IN

Chrysanthemum
Dahlia
Delphinium
Dianthus (carnation, pink)
Fuchsia
Hosta (plantain lily)
Iris
Lathyrus odoratus
(sweet pea)
Primula
Rosa (rose)

THE PLANT LOVER'S GARDEN

Although there is now an increasing trend for people to require low-maintenance gardens and easy-to-grow plants, there are still many people who love gardening and who do not want a low-maintenance garden. Growing plants is their life, and they want to use every available scrap of space for their passion.

It is surprising how many plants can be accommodated in a small garden. Such people enjoy the thought of growing things and of being in contact with nature, even in a limited way, and they enjoy working in the open air. They also enjoy the results that their efforts produce – a garden full of attractive plants and, if they also grow vegetables, fresh, tasty produce. There is no question that this is much harder work than looking after, say, a modern garden, which is mainly composed of hard surfaces, but then, to enjoy the cultivation of each plant is the whole point of it.

There is an increasing range of plants from which to choose. You can specialize, by growing, say, alpines, or hardy perennials, or even more specifically, roses, dahlias or fritillaries. Only a limited choice is available from general garden centres and nurseries, but there is a vast array of specialist nurseries that either provide plants at the nursery or supply them through mail order.

There are specialist societies, which promote their particular area of interest and often have seed exchange schemes that make available to members seeds of plants rarely seen elsewhere. Specialization is an exciting world, and a small garden is usually just the right size for a collection.

DESIGNING WITH PLANTS

Few of the gardeners who take time and trouble growing plants are happy to put them just anywhere in the garden. They like to create a pleasing scene, whether this is achieved in an *ad hoc* way, by buying or growing plants and just planting them where they seem to fit into a general design, or by adopting what many might regard as a more interesting and rewarding approach, by giving some thought to the overall planting scheme. The factors to consider are fundamental things such as when the plants flower and their colour, height, spread and shape. Although it can be fun to add a jarring note into a scheme, most prefer to create a wholly harmonious scene.

THINKING COLOUR

One of the most important aspects to consider is colour. Certain colours go together much more comfortably than others. Thus pastel shades blend well and create a peaceful, hazy atmosphere. Bright colours, on the other hand, are more vibrant and add a touch of excitement to a border. Other colours clash and should be avoided unless you deliberately want to make a statement – purple and orange or pink and orange, for example, make unhappy combinations. Other colours clash so much that it is worth using them occasionally just to pep things up. A bright yellow in a bright blue border, for example, or a splash of red against a green background will draw the eye.

SIZE AND SHAPE

A border of same-sized plants is visually boring, whereas one that includes variations in height will be much more interesting. The classic way to organize a border is to place the taller plants at the back and the shorter ones at the front, so that they build up in tiers. This kind of arrangement can be rather predictable and unexciting and can be relieved by pulling forward a few of the taller plants and allowing the shorter ones to grow towards the back. The shapes of different plants vary considerably and use should be made of this. Some lie flat, hugging the ground; others shoot up in narrow columns; some produce rounded shapes; and others are like fountains. All this variation should be taken advantage of to make your small garden as interesting as possible.

SILVER FOLIAGE

Artemisia 'Powis Castle'

Cerastium tomentosum (snow-in-summer)

Convolvulus cneorum

Cynara cardunculus (cardoon)

Eryngium giganteum
  (Miss Willmott's ghost)

Hebe pinguifolia 'Pagei'

Lavandula angustifolia

Pyrus salicifolia 'Pendula'

Santolina pinnata subsp. *neapolitana*

Stachys byzantina (lambs' ears)

GOLDEN FOLIAGE

Acer shirasawanum 'Aureum'

Fuchsia 'Golden Treasure'

Gleditsia triacanthos 'Sunburst'

Hedera helix 'Buttercup'

Hosta 'Sum and Substance'

Humulus lupulus 'Aureus' (golden hop)

Lonicera nitida 'Baggesen's Gold'

Lysimachia nummularia 'Aurea'

Milium effusum 'Aureum'
  (Bowles' golden grass)

Origanum vulgare 'Aureum'
  (golden wild marjoram)

THE FOLIAGE GARDEN

It is easy to think of gardens in terms of flowers rather than plants, but flowers can be time consuming to tend, so why not go for a foliage effect? More text more text more text more text more text more text more text more text more text more text.

A garden without flowers, or with only a few flowers, need never be dull. Foliage can provide all the interest you need. It may be only green, but you will quickly realize what a tremendous range of greens there is once you start to assemble them. In addition to the colours, there is the texture. Glossy leaves, for example, will illuminate dull corners by reflecting light, and thick, velvety ones will invite you to caress them. Then there is the variation in shapes. Tall rustling bamboos, low hummocks of moss, rounded clumps of hostas, fountains of cordylines, grass paths, yew hedges ... the possibilities are almost endless.

Foliage plants generally need far less attention than flowering ones – there are no dead flowers to remove for a start – and trees and shrubs also need far less maintenance, than say, herbaceous plants. Not all foliage plants are low maintenance, of course, but one in particular provides the last word in low-maintenance gardens.

THE ULTIMATE LOW-MAINTENANCE GARDEN

There are many people who would like to have a low-maintenance garden but do not want one that is covered in concrete. The next best thing is ivy (*Hedera helix*). Ivy makes the perfect ground cover. It will cover the soil and anything that gets in its way with a dense blanket of creeping stems and leaves. It works well in both shade and open sunlight and is particularly valuable for gardens that are shaded by adjacent building or trees.

First design the area, sculpting the ground with mounds and hollows, perhaps with a low earth wall or a shallow ditch. Place a few objects around, such as tree stumps or even low fences. Finally, plant as many ivies as you can afford – the cheapest way is to produce hundreds of plants from cuttings – and let them cover the whole area. It will climb over the humps and hollows and form a sculptural blanket. Variations can be introduced by using variegated ivies at strategic places or over particular features. The result is truly spectacular, individual and, of course, low maintenance, because all that is required is to clip it over once a year in early spring.

MOVING AWAY FROM GREEN

Not all foliage is green by any means. There are plants with dark, smoky purple leaves and those with dusky blue-grey leaves; there are plants with golden foliage and a large range that have variegated foliage. A garden devoted to any of these can easily become rather boring, as too many purples or blues tend to appear leaden and heavy, while a lot of variegated plants in one place tend to clash and become too 'busy', with nowhere for the eye to rest. Used as a contrast to, or occasional change from, green foliage, however, variegated plants come into their own.

Variegated foliage plants are the must numerous of the non-green types. At a distance they may seem the same, but start examining them closely and the variation becomes apparent. It may be in the colour, with a wide range of yellows, creams and silver as well as reds, purples and browns forming the contrasting colour to the basic green, but it may also be in the shape of the variegation, sometimes regular, sometimes not, or it may be its position, sometimes on the margin, sometimes towards the centre and sometimes seemingly random.

EXOTIC-LOOKING PLANTS

Bougainvillea glabra
Canna indica (Indian shot plant)
Coleus blumei (syn. *Solenostemon scutellarioides*)
Hibiscus rosa-sinensis (Rose of China)
Impatiens walleriana (busy Lizzie)
Ipomoea purpurea (morning glory)
Monstera deliciosa (Swiss cheese plant)
Musa basjoo (Japanese banana)
Nerium oleander (rose bay)
Passiflora caerulea (passion flower)

THE URBAN JUNGLE

The small garden is the perfect size for creating an exotic, jungle garden – an exciting place, surrounded by greenery and brightly-coloured flowers, with spaces to sit carved out in a jungle clearing. The overall effect is of lush green growth with occasional splashes of rich colour, which can be temporarily increased by bringing brightly coloured houseplants out in the open for special occasions.

Tropical plants are usually too tender to grow outside in more temperate climates, but there are sufficient plants with a tropical feel about them to create the impression of a jungle. The secret is to have plenty of large, exuberant plants, so that the space becomes overcrowded and jungle-like in feel. Large-leaved plants, such as bananas (*Musa*), and densely growing ones, such as bamboos, are ideal. The tropical image is enhanced by using brightly coloured flowers.

Bright reds and oranges, colours that stand out against the green background, are the types of colour to select. Cannas, which also have excellent 'jungle' foliage, are perfect plants for this type of garden, and they can be grown either in the ground or in containers. Many of the lilies will also serve the purpose. The tender bottlebrushes (*Callistemon*) are not tropical plants, but they have just the right feel. Daturas and brugmansias have more muted colours, but the size of their trumpet flowers makes up for this. Not all plants need to be tender, of course. The flowers of the more brightly coloured camellias set off against the gloss of the leathery leaves are perfect. Even humble plants like busy Lizzies (*Impatiens*), especially the dark-leaved forms, will add to the effect you are trying to create.

Climbing plants always add a vertical dimension to the garden. They are also useful for clothing the boundaries and adjacent buildings, providing a wall of greenery. Even more jungle-like are those that hang down in great swags, and these are especially useful for growing around pergolas and arbours. Most of the clematis are rather too bland to help achieve a tropical look, but jasmines can be used to clothe arches and arbours. The large-leaved ivies and the huge leaves of the vine *Vitis coignetiae* will all add to the general atmosphere, and the exotic flowers and thick foliage of the passion flowers (*Passiflora*) make these worth growing.

HARDY EXOTICA

The backbone of such a garden should be hardy plants so that they can stay outside all year round, but they can be supplemented by a selection of more exotic but tender species, which can be overwintered in a conservatory or greenhouse. Large-leaved plants, such as the rhubarbs (*Rheum*), rodgersias, phormiums and hostas, work well, as do many of the larger ferns. Bamboos are ideal because not only do they produce a thicket of growth, but they also rustle in an attractive way. Other grasses, especially the tall ones, such as miscanthus and the giant reed (*Arundo donax*), are good. The key to choosing the plants is that they should have a lush quality about them.

TENDER EXOTICA

There are a large number of more exotic plants that can be grown outside in summer but need to be given protection in winter, either in a conservatory or in a heated greenhouse. Bananas and rubber plants (*Ficus elastica*) are two obvious examples. Hibiscus, especially the red-flowered forms, is the perfect plant for the urban jungle, as is the flowering maple (*Abutilon*).

Many indoor plants enjoy a 'holiday' outside during the warm days of summer, and they can be used to heighten the exotic flavour of the garden. Especially useful are those with colourful foliage, such as the coleus, or the bromeliads with their bright red and yellow leaves. The curious flowers of the flamingo flower (*Anthurium*), the fiery bracts of the scarlet star (*Guzmania*) and the coloured foliage of the croton (*Codiaeum*) will all add to the scene. Such plants can be moved outside for the summer or just taken outdoors to enhance the effect for a special occasion. However, they should all be moved back indoors before the first frosts of autumn.

When you are using plants in pots, especially if the pots are more or less the same size, try to vary the height by standing them on plinths, consisting of one or two loose bricks. Above this height the plinth should be made more stable using cement.

PLANTS FOR A JAPANESE GARDEN

Acer palmatum (Japanese maple)
Bamboos
Chrysanthemum hortorum
  (syn. *Dendranthema grandiflorum*)
Iris ensata
Juniperus communis
Mosses
Paeonia suffruticosa
Pinus sylvestris (Scots pine)
Prunus mume (Japanese apricot)
Wisteria sinensis

JAPANESE STYLE

As in all aspects of our lives, travelling to other countries has influenced our gardens, but of all countries, Japan has probably had the greatest effect on garden design. The simplicity and tranquillity of the gardens there has been much copied in the West, often to great effect.

The essence of Japanese gardens is simplicity, which creates a sense of calm and peace. In today's hectic world any garden is a haven from the pressures and hurly-burly of day-to-day life, but a Japanese garden is entirely so. It is an area of total calm set around the house. One aspect of the simplicity is the limited use of materials and plants, and another is the way in which the available space is used. In the past every element in the garden was imbued with its own significance, and to some extent this is still true, but now the symbolism tends to be retained for largely historical reasons rather than because it has any real meaning.

Nature plays a dominant role in Japanese garden design. Everything seems to flow from it, especially the natural landscape. Instead of making miniature copies of the landscape as we might do in the West, however, Japanese design is suggestive. Where we might build, say, a rock garden, a Japanese gardener would use rocks and boulders to represent mountains or islands, while areas of raked gravel or sand are used to signify water. Closely clipped shrubs may be used to represent boulders, while small, carefully pruned trees are floating clouds. In nature there are rarely any straight lines, and so it is in the Japanese garden.

WATER

Streams and waterfalls are major landscape elements that are constantly used in Japanese gardens. They are usually imitations of natural streams, representing mountain torrents. Water is also present in the form of small pools or dishes of water, or water is introduced into the garden gently trickling through artificial courses, such as along split bamboo pipes. Sometimes the system is ingenious, with one pipe slowly filling before it tips and fills the next and so on. Everything is done with great simplicity. The water is calm or only just moving; there are no fountains to disturb the tranquillity. In addition to real water, there is much representational water in Japanese gardens. An area of raked gravel, for example, represents swirling water, while rounded rocks positioned on the gravel are islands set in the water. Often a ribbon of moss will pass through rocks and boulders, alluding to a stream

FLOWERS

Although several flowers are used in Japanese garden design, they never play a dominant role as they do in Western gardens. They, along with a few other plants, such as grasses, are used sparingly. The main flowering plants are chrysanthemums, irises, lilies and peonies. Trees and shrubs are widely used, especially around the perimeter of the garden to create a backdrop and to reinforce the idea of the 'borrowed landscape' beyond the confines of the garden itself. Within the garden, certain trees are valued, especially ancient ones. Pines, junipers and acers are particular favourites.

ORNAMENTS

A few ornaments are used within the garden, the best known of which is the Japanese lantern. These stone or metal lanterns, often like miniature buildings, are carefully positioned to illuminate key places along paths or water. They will often be placed next to water so that they produce reflections. Paths are of gravel or stone. Stepping stones are another popular feature, either made from slabs of stone or from sections of tree trunks. Bridges are often incorporated to cross either real or imaginary streams. In larger gardens there may be a pavilion or tea house, and a loggia may be built near the house from which the garden may be viewed.

BOUNDARY TREATMENTS

Window boxes, filled with annuals, can be used to draw attention away from an ugly wall or fence, or merely to decorate it. Hanging baskets can play a similar role.

In a small garden you are never far from the boundaries, which therefore play a much more significant role than they do in larger areas. Because they are so prominent they need attention, either to make them disappear into the background or to make a positive, interesting feature of them.

In the past boundaries, such as fences or walls, were there to keep out other people's animals and to keep in your own livestock. A boundary was also a way of marking the edge of your territory. It is still true, of course, that boundaries are used to restrain animals, but now it is pets rather than farm animals that we try to keep in or out of our gardens. There are other functions, too, of course. Keeping out unwanted people has become important, particularly in the search for privacy and security. Tall boundaries keep prying neighbours out and help to deflect sounds and smells, such as from traffic and barbecues. Fences and trellising can be used, but tall vegetation creates a thicker insulation between you and the outside world.

FORGIVE THE INTRUSION

Boundaries can be ugly and they can intrude into the garden. One way of coping with this is to disguise them. Using climbing plants is one solution, especially if you use something evergreen, such as ivy. This perhaps can, in turn, become boring, but the expanse of green can be enlivened by growing flowering plants such as honeysuckle and clematis through it to relieve it at different times of the year. Another solution is to paint the offending boundary, either so that it retires into the background – by painting it green, for example – or by jazzing it up with bright colours.

CREATING INTEREST

In small gardens every scrap of space should be used to its best advantage, and so, although you can disguise walls and fences, it does seem a pity to waste them. A lot can be done to enliven them and either make them a feature in their own right or use them as a prop for something more interesting. *Trompe-l'oeils*, for example, can be painted on the walls to make the garden seem larger than it actually is or just to provide visual interest. They can be hung with a variety of objects, plaques and plant containers. At one extreme there might be a bright mosaic, including glittering pieces of mirror, at the other a series of windowboxes filled with bright red geraniums might create the effect you want. Imagination is the keyword here.

STARTING FROM SCRATCH

Not all gardeners are lucky enough to have solid walls and fences, even ugly ones, marking their boundaries. They may have to start from scratch, either because there is nothing at all or because what there is is falling down and needs replacing. Instant solutions are found in the form of fences, which can be either see-through or solid panelling. Walls are the most attractive and desirable option, but they are expensive. Hedges can create an impenetrable barrier and absorb a certain amount of sound, but they take time to grow, and a useful rule of thumb to bear in mind is that the quicker the plants fill out into a hedge, the more frequently they will need clipping to keep them to the desired shape. Another possibility is to grow an informal hedge. This is a row of seemingly random plants, such as shrubs, that are not regularly clipped but allowed to grow to their natural shape. They are, however, planted close enough together to create a barrier.

PAINTING DULL WALLS

Walls and fences always sound desirable objects to have in a garden, but they often turn out to be pretty boring and have few redeeming features, apart from their ability to keep out the neighbours. A little judicious use of paint will, however, give them a new lease of life.

There may well also be functional reasons for painting a wall. Many small gardens, for example, tend to be shady and dark, sometimes even too dark to grow plants or ever to look attractive. Painting the walls white or another pale colour will help to reflect light into the space.

creating a background

In gardens where plants are the most important feature, walls and fences tend to be simply either a background to, or a support for, plants. A well-built brick wall is

perfect in its own right for this, but if the wall is constructed from ugly bricks or concrete blocks, it can detract from the plants. A way to deal with this is to paint it dark green. This will allow it to merge with the foliage and be far less conspicuous. Shades of blue-green are popular, and although they stand out a bit more than plain green, they can still be sympathetic tones to use with a wide range of plants.

brightening up the landscape

Plants may not be the dominant feature, either in the garden as a whole or in the vicinity of the wall. When this is the case, the wall can be treated in such a way that it becomes a positive feature. Depending on the mood you want to create, you can use soft or bright colours. It can be painted all one colour or it can be several, possibly in bands or in some other pattern. Colour can be used to pick out certain areas – for example, the wall may be mostly red, but a green patch may be used behind planters containing red geraniums.

Exterior paintwork is exposed to the weather and therefore needs to be repainted regularly to keep it in good condition. Garden walls and fences, however, are usually painted for decorative effect rather than to protect them, and so it does not matter if the pain becomes a little chipped or flaked. Indeed, this may be desirable, and the wall can be painted in such a manner that it looks as if it has not been painted for years. This distressed look can bring age and character to a setting.

putting on the paint

The type of paint you use depends on the effect you want to achieve. For a long-lasting cover you should use an exterior wall paint that contains sand to make it hard-wearing and weatherproof. This is rather conventional, however, and exterior paints are available in only a fairly limited range of colours, so for more decorative effects ordinary household paints can be used. Emulsion paints will not wear well in the open, although they are perfect if you want a weathered look. Oil-based gloss paints will last much longer but will need to be regularly repainted if you want to keep the wall looking pristine.

As with any painting job, the first task is to prepare the surface. Thoroughly clean it down. Brickwork can be brushed down with a wire brush. Unless you want a really perfect finish it is unlikely that you will need to fill any gaps, although if you do, you should make sure that you use an exterior filler that will withstand the weather rather than one normally used indoors. If the surface is dusty or flaky it will be necessary to seal it with an exterior sealant before painting. This will also help to prevent the wall from absorbing the paint like a sponge and therefore make the paint go further.

Although ordinary household paintbrushes can be used, a special masonry brush for applying paint to stone and brickwork will make it easier to get into all the pores and crevices. Paint on a dry day, preferably one on which there is no wind so that dust is not blown against the still-wet paint. Emulsion paints can be applied direct to the surface, but oil-based gloss paints will require primers and undercoats to make sure that the best possible adhesion is achieved.

MOSAICS FOR WALLS

Mosaics can be used to brighten up a wall as well as to give it intrinsic interest. A mosaic needs plenty of planning, imagination and a bold hand, but those who are willing to give it a try are likely to be rewarded with something that is truly unique to their garden.

Mosaics have been around for many centuries. They were originally mainly used for floor decoration and were made up of thousands of small coloured tiles or tesserae (singular tessera). These were made from fired clay. Tesserae are still available from craft and specialist suppliers and can be used for a mosaic in the classical style. There is, however, a much wider range of materials that can be used, and one of the best, as well as one of the cheapest, sources of supply is broken pottery. Fragments of white or brightly coloured ceramics are ideal for creating a modern mosaic. Pieces of old tiles can also be used, as can coloured glass, including pieces from broken bottles. The mosaic could also contain three-dimensional objects, such as shells and pebbles.

Opposite: Mosaics can be
great fun to construct and
provide colour in the garden.

playing with light

Although a mosaic can be placed against any background, it is worth considering its placement and adapting the design if necessary so that it is seen to its best advantage. Some of the brightest and most eye-catching mosaics are seen in Mediterranean countries, where the colours are set off against white-painted walls. The white surround seems to illuminate the mosaic. Much pottery has a shiny glaze, and when shards of this are used light is reflected back from the mosaic itself, usually changing as the sunlight changes throughout the day or even when it is seen from a different viewpoint, because the tiny pieces are set into the pattern at slightly different angles. To make the most of reflected light, small pieces of mirror or glass can also be used.

searching for inspiration

Some people are able to create artworks, including mosaics, straight from their heads. Most of use, however, need some form of help or inspiration. The first thing is to decide what style the mosaic should have – classical, abstract or figurative, for example, or perhaps it should be related to gardens or gardening or to the family in some way. The next step is to look at examples. Illustrations of classical mosaics are readily available in books and magazines, and there are many books on art and design containing examples of other styles. With a bit of thought it is possible to create your own design.

Abstract schemes are probably the easiest, especially if you choose a geometric pattern, but you could select a freestyle arrangement with swirls of colour. If you want a blaze of colour, you could always cover the whole area either in random pieces or in, say, pieces in different shades of green, perhaps mixed with a few fragments of yellow. If you are more confident about your skills, you might prefer to copy a picture or photograph, rather as you would create a cross-stitch pattern. Draw a grid on the original picture and use this to transfer the outlines and colours to the wall bearing a similar, but enlarged grid.

picking up the pieces

The wall on which the mosaic is to be created should be sound and preferably flat, unless, of course, you want to make a three-dimensional mosaic, which can look striking on a wall; if you want to do this, sculpt the wall to the required shape before starting the mosaic. Because the mosaic will be out in all weathers it must be weatherproof, so use cement rather than an indoor adhesive for attaching the pieces to the wall. The grouting between the pieces should also be waterproof and should fill all the gaps and crevices so that no water can get into the design. If water does work its way between pieces of the pattern, it may freeze in winter and in doing so expand and force the piece away from the wall.

1
Brush the wall thoroughly to remove any loose material then wash to remove dirt.

2
Draw the pattern on to the wall and apply a small area of adhesive and stick on pieces of tile.

3
When all the tiles are in place, rub over with a waterproof grout, wiping off the excess before it sets.

APPLYING MOSAICS

Before you begin, brush down the wall to remove any loose pieces of material and all dust. If the wall is uneven and you want a perfectly smooth finish to the mosaic, it may be necessary to render the area with cement. Seal the brickwork with a sealant that is sold as being suitable for outside walls. If you have worked out a design on paper, transfer the outline to the wall to the appropriate scale. Use a tile cutter to cut the pieces of old pottery, tile, glass, mirror or shell to size and shape, then use a tile adhesive to stick the pieces to the wall in the appropriate positions. Rub grout all over the mosaic, filling in all the gaps. Thoroughly wipe off all the excess from the surface of the mosaic before it sets.

WALL DECORATIONS

Walls inside a house cry out for decoration — and so do those on the outside. All manner of objects can be used to enhance them. Unlike paint and most mosaics, objects can be used to create three-dimensional effects, in which the play of light and shade is an important factor in the overall appearance.

A wall can be used as a gallery for objects: items that have been collected over the years or that you have found and want to keep as a memento or that suddenly take your fancy. They can be as ephemeral as a piece of dead branch or they can be a relic of the past, such as an old iron bicycle frame or the end of a bed. The objects could be related – a collection of old horticultural tools, for example, would be appropriate in a garden. The subject depends on your taste, but often objects of this sort look better if they appear to have been left hanging, almost accidentally, where they are now found – as if they were last used years before and simply overlooked – than if they seem to have been only recently put on display.

plaques and masks

Although bizarre objects can be amusing, they are not to everybody's taste. Many feel that terracotta plaques or face masks are more in keeping with a garden setting. There is a large range of both of these, as well as cement and stone-substitute versions, available from garden centres and other specialist outlets. Sometimes the subject is of classical origin; sometimes it may be something simple, such as a lion's head.

high-rise plants

The term windowboxes suggests that such containers should be used only on windowsills, but there is no reason why they should not be attached to a blank wall or fence. Boxes in neat rows or at staggered intervals or perhaps even placed at random, all filled with, say, bright red geraniums or tumbling petunias, will transform the ugliest of walls. As well as full-sized boxes, there are a number of smaller wall planters in which you can either plant directly or insert plants in a flowerpot. These can be mixed with larger boxes to introduce greater variety.

Containers of this sort will need watering at least once a day, perhaps twice a day, during hot, sunny weather. Unless you have some means of reaching the upper ones, do not place containers higher on the wall than you can comfortably reach with a watering can full of water. You can buy special pump-action watering cans with a long nozzle for reaching hanging baskets, which can also be used for this purpose. Excess water will often trickle out of the containers and down the wall, leaving a dirty stain, so do not use them if this matters. Water may also penetrate a single-skinned wall, leaving a stain on the inside if it is a wall of a house.

waterspouts

If you have no room for a pond in the garden, a waterspout attached to the wall with the water tumbling into a small pool may be most welcome. If there are children around, this type of arrangement makes it possible for you to have water in the garden without the risks associated with an open pond, because the water can fall between stones with the reservoir safely tucked away below ground level.

Below: Many different objects can be used to decorate a wall. Here a small fountain adds sound as well as beauty to the scene.

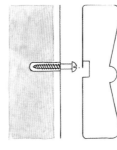

1

Drill a hole into the wall, plug it, and screw in a screw to hang the object from.

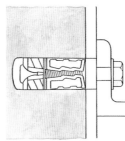

2

Heavy objects can be fixed directly to the wall by drilling a hole and then using an expanding bolt.

3

Light plaster objects can be stuck to the wall with adhesive. Hold the object in place with tape or pins until it has set.

FIXING DECORATIONS TO WALLS

Many objects can be nailed directly to the wall or fence. Use masonry nails for brick, but wear protective goggles because they can sometimes shatter violently as you strike them. For other surfaces it may be necessary to drill and plug a hole before using screws or expanding bolts to make a more permanent fixing. Make certain the object is well fixed so that it cannot fall or be blown off the wall.

Unless you want the mask or plaque to be loose so that you can take it with you if you move house, the best way of fixing this type of object to a wall is with cement. Make sure that you have some method of supporting the plaque until the cement has set or you may find that it falls off when the still-wet cement slowly slumps. For loose fixing, use screws or bolts as described above.

STYLISH FENCES

Fences can be cheaply and quickly erected, creating an almost instant boundary. The days are long gone when a fence consisted of nothing more than a few strands of wire stretched between posts. These days, a wide range of styles and materials is available, and with a little imagination you can make something that is unique to your own garden.

WILLOW HEDGES

If you can obtain freshly cut wands of willow (*Salix*), use them as hardwood cuttings and plant them straight into the ground between late autumn and early spring. An alternative, but much more expensive, option is to buy individual willow plants and reduce them to four stems. Place four cuttings next to each other in a line at intervals of 20cm (8in), arranging them so that two slope one way and two the other. Weave each pair in and out of others so that an open, diamond pattern is created. Cut off the tops at the required height and weave several extra wands horizontally along the top to hold the whole together.

The wands will take root, and side shoots and leaves will appear. Once a year, in spring, remove all side shoots. The wands will eventually graft themselves together to create a strong, living hurdle, and as long as the side shoots are removed each year, it will retain its appearance without turning into a hedge.

Traditional fences often consisted of posts with single wires or wooden rails between them. These are efficient for marking the boundary, but they are not of much use for keeping out people or animals or for creating privacy. Hanging wire-netting between the posts overcomes part of the problem: it is relatively cheap but is far from beautiful. It is possible to improve things somewhat by alternating different panels of netting, perhaps turning some at 45 or 90 degrees to give variations in the pattern. An alternative solution is to disguise an old wire fence with a fedge, a combination of a fence and a hedge. All you do is plant ivy along the fence so that it climbs up and covers the wire. It creates a narrow hedge than only needs trimming once a year, if that (see page 104).

wooden alternative

In small town gardens wooden panel fences are popular. There are various styles to choose from. Some are cheap, look cheap and rarely last long. Others, usually more expensive, not only look more solid but actually last much longer and are worth the extra investment. Nevertheless, despite looking worthy, these are still rather dull. Even when they are enlivened by having trellis attached to the top, they still look rather run of the mill.

bringing in the countryside

A touch of the countryside can be introduced by using traditional hurdles, of the kind that were originally made for enclosing sheep or cattle. These panels, which are made up of woven hazel or willow, are usually decorative. The craft of hurdle-making is increasingly being revived for the garden market, and more and more individual designs are becoming available. Some of the open-weave panels are attractive and suitable for internal screens, although they are not practical for external boundaries.

Willow, in particular, is becoming more generally available, and there is no reason why you should not make living hurdles to your own design.

bamboo

One way of getting something more individual is to make your own fence. There are several ways of doing this, some having a more obviously do-it-yourself look than others. Bamboo fences provide a sympathetic backdrop in a small garden, and the simplest way to create a screen is to nail a roll of bamboo matting over an existing fence. It is best if only the framework of the fence is used so that light filters between the individual canes, but it can still be used over a solid fence to disguise it as long as none of the original fence is visible. Larger canes can be individually nailed to wooden rails held between posts. The canes can vary in thickness to provide interest, being placed either in a regular pattern or at random. Similarly, the height of individual canes can vary.

solid wood

Solid wood can make an excellent fence, capable of surviving event the harshest of weather conditions. Picket fences have a particular charm, which goes especially

well with small gardens, particularly if the house is old. The fence consist of flat
pieces of wood, each about 5cm (2in) wide, nailed to two or three horizontal rails,
which, in turn, are held in position by posts set at 1.8m (6ft) intervals. There is
usually a gap between the slats the same width as the slats themselves. The tops
of individual pickets are shaped in various ways – cut to a point, rounded
or shaped in a circle, for example. The slats are often painted white, but they can
be left natural or painted a soft blue-green.

ENTRANCES AND EXITS

Entrances and exits are important parts of any garden. Not only do they provide security but they are also the visual threshold to your garden, the first and last places that people see when they visit. Their appearance, therefore, tends to create a lasting impression of your garden.

Consider the view framed by the entrance. It may be the path and front door or it may be the garden itself. No matter what is framed, it gives an immediate impression of your space. A complete archway, whether it is solidly made of brick, wood or iron, or living, in the form of a hedge, is the best sort of frame. Stand at the entrance to your own garden and think about the impression you want to give.

archways

Archways are the ultimate way of framing entrances and exits as well as of linking different areas of the garden. A glimpse of what lies beyond is often tantalizing enough for people to abandon the area they are in and move on to the next. The simplest way of creating an archway is to buy one of the many plastic or metal ones that are available from garden centres and the larger DIY stores. Plastic usually looks like plastic and does not last long, so metal is a more economical choice for the long term. Many of the ready-made arches are too narrow. When you are buying an arch, always imagine what it will be like when it is covered with roses and how little space will be left between the posts for you to pass comfortably through and under it.

clothing the arch

Depending on its situation, it may be best to leave the arch unclothed. In a small garden, however, where space is at a premium, an archway can be used as an excuse to grow a few more plants, climbing ones in this case. Roses are popular choices for this type of situation, and you may want to look for a thornless variety, such as *Rosa* 'Zéphirine Drouhin'. Many roses will produce flowers all summer through, but by running a clematis up through the rose you make sure of a double season. Both the rose and the clematis should be planted in spring and tied in to the uprights. Keep the shoots inside the arch trimmed or tied back so that the plants do not become an obstacle.

gates

There is a wide range of gates available, made of metal or wood. Metal gates with widely spaced bars may pose a security risk if there are young children in the garden (see below), but whatever material and style you choose, make sure that the uprights are well concreted in or they will soon move and the gate will stick or constantly swing open. Internal gateways can be more frivolous. They need not even be designed to shut but can be used to draw the eye to another part of the garden or become a focal point in their own right.

security

Security is a tedious but, unfortunately, necessary consideration. You can adopt a cavalier attitude towards keeping intruders out, but if you have children it is essential that there are adequate, safe gates through which they cannot slip. Secure out-of-reach catches are essential. Self-closing devices are useful to make sure that gates shut after visitors, such as the postman. Unfortunately, they can compound the problem, because if a child does manage to slip out they can't slip in again.

1
Lay the elements out on the ground, cutting V-joints in the uprights and the corresponding noses in the cross pieces.

2
Nail the elements together securely, from the outside of the uprights into the cross pieces, using galvanized nails.

Opposite: Rather than make a proper archway, a simple tripod or column can be constructed and placed on either side of an entrance.

Below: One of the simplest ways of creating an entrance is to allow the upper part of a hedge to grow across a gap to form an archway.

3
Erect the upright panels by concreting them into holes in the ground. Fix the top panel in place to create the arch.

MAKING A RUSTIC ARCH

Making your own arch is often cheaper than buying a ready-made one from a garden centre, and it can be more fun and certainly more rewarding. The simplest style is a rustic archway, because any imprecise cutting or jointing will not be noticeable. Sweet chestnut poles are the most satisfactory type of wood, but any timber that has been treated with preservative can be used. It is important that the base of each upright is well buried, preferably in concrete, because when the arch is clothed with climbers the wind pressure is enormous and an insecure arch will soon topple over.

For a simple arch, four uprights will be needed. Use galvanized nails to attach two or three horizontal bars between the side uprights and two horizontal crossbars across the top between the two sides. Nail three more bars between the top crossbars. Alternatively, use shorter crossbars, nailed at a 40 degree angle to create a triangular top to the arch.

INSPIRED LANDSCAPES

Most small gardens are hard-working areas, which are used for a wide variety of outdoor activities. The days when a garden was used exclusively for growing plants are long gone, and most people now want gardens that have an area that is paved in some way to provide plenty of space on which tables and chairs can be used for meals and entertaining, as well as having barbecues, sunbathing and for the children to play on.

GETTING IT RIGHT

Although most surfaces can, as long as they are not concreted down, be moved, it is a difficult and expensive job. It is important, therefore, to be certain that you get it right first time. Take your time to plan the area. Draw it out on paper. Outline it on the ground and take time to walk around the area, viewing it in your mind's eye to check that it is right before you start. If you are uncertain, consider a few alternative ideas before you definitely commit yourself, and if at all possible, visit gardens where different types of surface can be seen in *situ*.

USING GRASS

In the past such spaces were usually put down to grass, and there is no reason why this should not still be so. There are tough grasses that will withstand children's play and the regular passage of feet along paths, just as there are softer grasses that are aesthetically more pleasing if you like perfect lawns. The two main disadvantages of grass are that it cannot be used in winter and it needs cutting. This last characteristic – that grass needs cutting – means that you need somewhere to keep the mower and somewhere to put the cuttings, even if only temporarily before taking them to the tip. These requirements place demands on a garden that may already be short of space and on a gardener who may be short of time. Even given these drawbacks, however, lawns have many benefits and are still perfect places for relaxing on a summer day.

HARD SURFACES

If you decide against grass, there are plenty of other surfaces from which to choose. Most are far more expensive in the short term, but they are easy to maintain, do not need a lawnmower and can be used in winter. Paving slabs are possibly the easiest to deal with, and results are almost immediately apparent. Bricks and pavers are the other most often used hard surfacing materials, and they provide an attractive, albeit expensive, surface.

SOFTER SURFACES

Anyone who falls on gravel will say that it is far from soft, but it is softer to look at than solid paving and can be quite flexible. It is relatively cheap and very quick to lay, and the results are pleasing as long as it is regularly raked and weeds are removed. Gravel is available in a range of sizes and colours, and it works well when it is used in combination with other materials – slab stepping stones, for example. Gravel is, however, mobile and must be contained by edging stones or boards of some sort so that it does not disappear into the borders or the lawn.

The softest surface is wood chippings. A deep layer of this in a children's play area will help to prevent many nasty bruises, grazes and knocks. It needs to be topped up from time to time and should be kept weed free.

ABOVE IT ALL

A less conventional way of creating a surface is to ignore the ground altogether and build a deck. This is, in effect, a wooden platform, which can be positioned on the ground or at some height above it. Decks are particularly useful for creating level surfaces in a garden that slopes (see pages 42–3).

PRETTY PAVING

If it suits your mood and the style of the garden, straightforward, four-square paving slabs, which are quick and easy to lay, are the obvious choice, but there are so many variations available that you can probably devise an original and interesting arrangement.

If you want to use basic slabs, consider laying them in an alternative to the conventional grid pattern. One option is simply to stagger them or turn them through 45 degrees so that they make a diagonal pattern – a simple but attractive alternative. Another possibility is to use a combination of different-size slabs. This needs careful planning or you will find you have too many of some slabs and not enough of another. Carefully work out the layout on paper before you begin.

Another simple but effective way of ringing the changes is to use coloured or textured slabs. Textured slabs now come in a wide variety of patterns. Some are simply the uneven surface of riven stone, but others are imitations of other paving methods, such as stable bricks. These can be arranged in circular patterns as well

Opposite left: Paving slabs do not have to look severe. Here they have been used in a stepped fashion to create an interesting pattern.

Opposite right: Patterns can be created by using concentric circles of differing materials. You may have to cast difficult patterns yourself.

as the more conventional squares. The slabs can be made more interesting if you cast them yourself. This gives you the opportunity not only to make different shapes but also to incorporate things like shells, pebbles or objects in the surface.

bricks and pavers

Bricks are a traditional form of paving or hard surface, but, like all good materials, they transcend their age and still have the ability to look modern and stylish. This is partly because they are versatile and can be laid in a wide variety of patterns, especially if you mix colours and textures. This characteristic makes it possible for anyone who wants to do so to create an individual shape and pattern for their patio and paths. Bricks tend to be slightly irregular, both in shape and colour, whereas pavers are much more regular in both respects and have a more modern, streamlined feel.

Both can be laid on a bed of sand in the same way as paving slabs, but for heavy use, especially if they are to be used as a drive, an underlying layer of concrete should be laid first. Hiring an impactor will help to compact the soil beneath the area to be covered as well as to make sure that all the bricks or pavers are tamped down into the sand, creating a perfectly level surface.

mixing it

Mixing different media always produces a much more interesting surface. Paving slabs, especially stone ones if you can afford them, work well with traditional bricks as well as with gravel or larger stones, in the form of pebbles. Patterns can be created in the surface with flat pieces of tile, or tiles or slate stood on edge. Such decorative effects often produce a somewhat irregular surface to walk on and so should be used only in areas that are not much used for walking. They are, however, ideal for use as guides to indicate a path across a patio or as ornamental 'tram lines' on a path.

making your own

If you have the time it can be worth making your own slabs. This gives you an opportunity not only of using imaginative shapes but also rendering or colouring the surface in a variety of ways. Pebbles, pieces of mosaic or old brick – more or less anything you wish, in fact – can be added to the surface of the concrete. If the concrete is brushed before it is fully cured – that is, it is still soft – the aggregate (stones) will be exposed, giving the slab an interesting finish.

non-mow grass

If a low-maintenance surface is a high priority for you, an area that is worth exploring is that of artificial grass, not the sort you see on greengrocers' stalls but the material that is used for all-weather sports surfaces. This can be laid over an existing terrace, although a smooth surface without cracks is really needed.

1

Make sure the area is flat and then lay down some sand and level it off.

2

Lay the slabs directly onto the sand, making certain that they are square to each other.

3

If necessary, add some more sand to make the slabs level with their neighbours.

4

Tap firmly into position, checking that they are level using a spirit level.

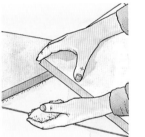

LAYING SLABS

Make sure that the area to be paved is level and compacted. If necessary, dig out soil to achieve the appropriate final level. Cover the area with a 5cm (2in) layer of sand and lay the slabs on top of this. Gently but firmly tap them to settle them into the sand. Adjust the amount of sand under each slab if necessary to produce a level surface, but remember that there should be a very slight slope in one direction to allow water to drain away.

If the soil is loose dig out about 15cm (6in), compact the base and add a 5–10cm (2–4in) layer of rubble. Compact this, then cover it with a layer of sand before continuing as above.

WORKING WITH LEVELS

A garden that slopes or is on different levels requires more planning and work to get the structure right, but once it is done, the difference in levels can produce a much more interesting garden than one on the flat. On the other hand, a level garden is much easier to work and move about on, especially for elderly or infirm gardeners.

RETAINING WALLS

In order to create two flat areas from a slope you will need to build a retaining wall between them. The wall can be of the dry-stone type or built from brick or blocks. Unless you are skilled in this type of work, however, it may be safer to employ a professional, because retaining walls have to withstand great pressure. It is essential that proper foundations are dug and filled with concrete before the wall is erected. For walls up to 60cm (2ft) high, the foundations should be 35cm (14in) deep with 15cm (6in) of concrete; for wall that are higher than this, the concrete should be 25cm (10in) deep. Brick and block walls will need a mortar bonding and weep holes should be left in the base of this to allow water to run out from behind the wall. Fill the space between the wall and the bank with a layer of rubble to aid drainage before backfilling with soil.

Needless to say there are many ways of coping with a slope, depending on the kind of space you want to create. If your garden is on a gentle slope, it may be easiest simply to ignore it. On the other hand, standing on a slope or constantly walking up or down can be tiring, and a whole garden on a slope rarely works visually. The solution to this is to remove the slope and to make two or more flat areas with steps between. In a small garden the upper level could be a terrace, especially if it is immediately outside the house, while the lower level becomes the lawn and flower and vegetable beds.

A more complicated approach is to remove the main slope and turn it into a series of level areas and random slopes. This makes a much less formal picture and can be quite exciting, especially if you prefer a more informal style of gardening. Yet another idea is to have a series of terraces, and this arrangement works especially well if the slope is steep, giving a series of level or gently sloping paths across the slope, each one backed by a wall or deep bed, which is tended from the path.

terracing a slope

When you are terracing a slope it is important to remember not to get topsoil and subsoil mixed up. The last thing you want is heavy clay sitting on top of fertile topsoil.

On a shallow slope with a reasonable depth of good soil it is possible to adjust the slopes simply by moving the soil around. If the slope is pronounced, however, hire a digger to help you move the soil. There are small, self-drive ones that will pass down the side of a house on a relatively narrow path. Push all the topsoil to one side and sculpt the ground as you want it before replacing the topsoil. This can be done by hand with a spade and wheelbarrow, but it is hard work.

moving water

A major advantage – indeed, one of the attractions – of having a sloping garden is that you can create convincing streams and waterfalls. The steeper the garden the more dramatic the water, which can descend from a 'spring' or a pool at the top and fall or run to a pool at the bottom, from whence it is pumped back to the top. The stream can be lined with concrete or a pond liner, but if you use a liner, make sure that it is hidden or completely disguised.

moving about

When your garden is arranged on more than one level, it is necessary to have a means of moving from one area to another. It is possible to build steps, but it may also be necessary to build a ramp so that you can easily move things like wheelbarrows and lawnmowers about. Bear in mind, too, that flights of shallow steps are not comfortable to ascend or descend. A ramp is a much better idea for such areas.

Steps must be solidly constructed. The style will largely depend on the style of the garden – formal steps will look out of place in an informal garden, for example – and this will also dictate your choice of material, from bricks, stone, concrete and wood.

Below: Informal steps are attractive and add charm and unique character to a garden.

Bottom: This striking water feature makes full use of changes of level in the garden.

Right: Normal steps are more practical if a path is used frequently. Trim plants back.

FLOORING IT OVER – DECKING

In many countries wooden decking is the preferred method of creating a sitting area. It is a natural extension of the idea of having a veranda running along the back of a house. These days, a deck can be built anywhere in the garden and does not have to be adjacent to the house.

The main advantage of decks is that because they are built from wood they can be constructed anywhere. There is no need to level the ground and no need to disturb the surrounding garden. They can also be built at almost any height, from ground to roof level. They can jut out from a high point in the garden to create a viewing platform or they can jut out over a pond, so that you can lie on the edge and watch the fish. They also have the advantage of being hard, so they do not wash away, do not need mowing and can be swept easily. At the same time they are relatively soft and yielding, unlike concrete, brick and stone. Wood will deteriorate with time, of course, but provided it is maintained regularly, it should last for many years.

Decking should be laid on
joists that themselves are
held above soil level to
prevent them from rotting.

Alternatively, they can be
laid on concrete joists or
even pillars if the ground
is sloping.

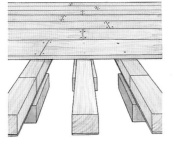

LAYING DECKING

The surface may consist of planks of wood that are butted close together to form a continuous surface or it may be formed from planks with gaps between them so that water can easily run away. Avoid laying a deck with wide gaps between the planks. Chair legs will tip into the spaces, and small articles will constantly drop between the planks, perhaps into an area from which they cannot easily be retrieved. In addition, children could easily get their feet trapped or twisted. It may seem to be a way of saving costs because it will obviously use less wood, but such a decking might well create more problems than it solves. Gaps of about 6mm (¹⁄₄in) are probably acceptable, and if the wood has not been thoroughly seasoned before it is laid, gaps of this size are likely to occur naturally as the wood dries out. The way the wood is laid is important because it will dictate the appearance of the deck. There is a wide range of patterns to choose from, including those that look like enlarged versions of interior woodblock flooring. The best wood is hardwood. It is solid, does not splinter and is less prone to rot. It can, however, be costly, especially if a large area is to be covered. Softwood, on the other hand, is much less expensive, but it can leave splinters in bare feet unless it is well prepared. It should be tanalized (treated with preservative) to prevent rotting, and the fixings, such as nails, bolts and screws, should be galvanized to prevent them from rusting.

shapes

Many decks are just square or rectangular simply because they are the easiest shapes to make. If the decking is going to fit comfortably in the overall garden design, however, it should fit the available space whatever that may be, even if this means spending extra time or money in getting it right.

Because wood comes in long planks and strips, one tends to think of things made of it as being composed of straight lines. Most decking has got a straight edge, but there is no reason why it should not be cut to make curves. A series of circles, perhaps at different levels, for example, could be extremely attractive, or the edge between the deck and a shrubbery or lawn could consist of a long sinuous line.

Because wood can be cut and shaped, holes can be made in the deck through which plants can grow. It would be possible to create a space or spaces for one or more small beds, perhaps with foliage plants or bushes growing in them, and it also means that established trees or bushes that are growing in the area that is to be covered by decking need not cut down: simply work around them. This approach can be effective on steeply sloping ground, where the deck might jut out high in the tops of the trees growing below, and it could be equally effective on level ground, where the trees will provide natural shade.

roofing it in

While trees make a natural canopy, it is possible to build a slatted roof over the decked area, which would let in a certain amount of light but filter out the sun. It could be constructed in such a way that an awning could be pulled over it to provide additional shade. Another possibility would be to build a pergola over all or part of the deck and grow climbing plants over it to provide shade, colour and perhaps perfume, depending on which plants you choose. Grape vines (*Vitis*) produce a wonderfully dappled light, which is perfect for eating under.

Opposite: Decking is a
wonderful way of creating a
sitting and entertaining area
in the garden. They can be
sophisticated, and almost
seem to be an extension of
the inside floors.

FROM HERE TO THERE – PATHS

It goes without saying that paths are an extremely important element in any garden. They serve both a practical and visual role and should be considered seriously when the garden is first laid out. Both the range of materials that can be used and the effect they can have on the garden are huge.

The prime function of any path is, of course, to get a person from A to B. This may seem an obvious statement, but it is a point that is often overlooked when gardens are laid out. Too often a major, much-used path meanders around a garden or has a dog-leg bend in it rather than going straight to its destination. The result is that people take short cuts, wearing patches in the lawn or jumping over borders so that they can get to their destination in the shortest possible time. When a path is going to be used a great deal – for example, if it leads to the front door – make it as straight and as direct as possible. Not all paths are major ones, of course; some are for more general access only – they might, for instance, go between or through borders or wind among shrubs. This kind of path can be as twisty and curved as you like because the people using it are rarely in a hurry; their purpose is not to get to the far end of the path but somewhere along it.

appearance matters

Paths create lines and ribbons in a garden, and the eye has a natural tendency to follow them. A straight path with, say, a shed at the end of it will quickly take the eye along it and come to a dead end. On the other hand, a path that curves will not only display what lies on each side of it, distracting the eye (which is, after all, one of the reasons for creating borders) but will also create a sense of mystery when it turns out of sight. Paths that disappear around a bend tend to draw the viewer on. In a small garden it is especially valuable to be able to give the impression that something lies beyond what is immediately visible and that the garden is much larger than it actually is.

material matters

A wide range of materials can be used for paths. If there are paved areas in other parts of the garden, using a similar material for the paths could help bring a feeling of unity. It might, on the other hand, be more interesting to use different, perhaps contrasting, materials, and this is particularly true if the paved area also serves as part of the path. For example, a path from a kitchen door might go across a terrace before proceeding to a vegetable plot. If the patio had a surface of paving stones, it would be visually interesting if the entire path, including the section that crossed the patio, were in brick.

As we have noted (see pages 38–9), paving slabs are relatively easy to lay. Brick is more expensive but good to look at, although brick paths can become slippery if they are covered with algae. Gravel paths are attractive as well as being cheap and easy to lay. Grass paths are also cheap and attractive, but they need mowing and cannot be used in wet weather or in winter without damaging the surface. Wood chippings make a soft path, but it will quickly begin to look untidy, and such paths are best confined to areas between trees and shrubs where grass will not grow and where this type of surface will look more natural.

There is no reason why several different materials should not be mixed. Paving slabs surrounded by gravel, for example, always look good. Bricks and granite setts are good companions for slabs or gravel.

Brick paths can be extremely attractive, but when in the shade of plants they can become very slippery with algae.

LAYING A BRICK PATH

Dig out the area of the path so that the final level will be just above the surrounding soil. Compact the soil at the bottom of the trench and put in a 5–10cm (2–4in) layer of rubble. Cover this with 5cm (2in) of concrete. The bricks can be laid on a thin bed of sand on top of the concrete, or they can be cemented in position. A concrete base is necessary for most well-used paths; otherwise they are likely to subside and become uneven. For little-used paths or for areas where the soil is already compacted, however, the bricks can be laid on sand directly on top of the compacted earth.

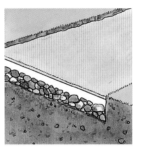

1

Bricks are best laid on a solid base of concrete, which in turn, has been laid on compacted hardcore.

2

Place a layer of sand on the base and then lay the bricks in the desired pattern.

3

Tap the bricks level, checking with a spirit level. Brush sand into the joints.

stepping stones

Stepping stones will often do just as well as a path. Stone slabs set in grass, for example, will preserve the visual quality of grass but at the same time provide a more hard-wearing surface. It is not always necessary to lay access paths through borders, where a few stepping stones will serve the purpose just as well and have the advantage that they can be easily moved if necessary.

ON EDGE – EDGING FOR PATHS, PATIOS AND BORDERS

Just as gardens need a boundary and pictures need a frame, most patios and paths need edging, for without it they are likely to merge into their surroundings. Sometimes this is just what you want, of course, but a distinct edge is usually more satisfactory.

An attractive edge to a path can be made by digging a shallow trench and then cementing bricks at a 45 degree angle.

EDGING A PATH

Hard edges can be rather severe – concrete kerbing, for example – or more relaxed looking – bricks, for example. Bricks can be run on the level, but they are often used on edge or emerging from the ground at an angle of 45 degrees. There are also a number of decorative or plain edging tiles, made from terracotta or cement. All of these are best cemented into place so that they are firmly embedded and help to support the edge of the path.

Dig a narrow trench along the line of the edging, put a layer of cement in the bottom and position the edging in it. For a heavily used area, such as along a drive, a deeper layer of concrete will make the edge more secure.

Edges serve two basic purposes. The first is to contain the path or patio physically; the second is to contain it visually. From the physical point of view an edge is mainly needed for loose fillings, such as gravel or bark, which can easily spill over into the border or lawn. Even hard surfaces benefit from having an edge, however, because it will help prevent the edge of the path from slumping and will also encourage traffic to keep on the path rather than running over into the border. A high edging will also help keep some of the taller border plants under control and stop them spreading over the path.

In visual terms, an edge or edging to a path helps to contain it, defining the boundary and guiding the eye along it. It can also be a decorative feature and will often act as the finishing touch.

soft option

Softer-looking edges can be made from more natural or organic materials. These may range from running a strip of grass along either side of paving, to using things like hoops bent from pliable sticks or lengths of metal, and hurdles or logs. Hoops and hurdles are ideal along the side of a border because they will prevent plants from flopping over the path or lawn. Log edging is ideal for a path of chipped bark, partly because their size helps retain the bark on the path and partly because the logs and the bark look like natural companions, especially in a shrubby or tree setting.

A positive edge to paths and borders can be created by using a low-growing hedge, and those formed of box (*Buxus sempervirens*) look especially attractive. They provide a barrier without totally separating the two areas, keeping the path from the border yet permitting the two areas to relate to each other. Keep such hedges clipped tight so that they always look neat.

lawns

Lawns normally just finish; there is no other edging material. There are times, however, when an edging is useful. Some gardeners like to lay a narrow row of paving slabs around a lawn, partly to obviate the need to cut the edges and partly to allow plants to flop over from the border without ruining the grass. Such an edging should be level with the lawn.

higher thoughts

The junction between a patio and the rest of the garden can be a difficult transitional area. So often the hard surface simply ends, and the garden starts in a rather unsatisfactory way. One way of make a positive termination of one and beginning of the other is to edge the patio with a low wall. This can simply be a brick or block wall, or it can be a raised bed built at the edge of the patio so that plants can be grown in it. Leave drainage holes in the side of the brickwork so that excess water can drain out of the bed into the garden.

Below: Plants make an effective edge. However they should not be allowed to overlap grass as it makes it difficult to mow and can kill patches of it.

Bottom: Plants are ideal for edging paths, softening edges and providing interest. Allow extra width for this when constructing paths.

ENHANCING THE SPACE

Space is always at a premium in small gardens and every opportunity should be taken to make a garden look and feel bigger than it actually is, even if it is only an illusion. One of the great frustrations of a small garden is that it usually looks precisely that: small. This generally affects the gardener in one of two ways. The first is the practical fact that there is a limit to what you can do in the area: the number of activities you carry out and the number of plants you grow will have to be restricted to the available space. The other problem is more psychological, in that the garden looks small and feels cramped.

PHYSICAL SIZE

If you are interested in growing plants there are one or two things you can do to squeeze a little more usable space out of a garden. The first is to use all the walls and grow vertically. You can attach window-boxes and other containers to walls to grow plants that you would normally grow in the soil, and to increase the amount of usable space it is possible to build a raised deck as a patio and use the area below the deck for storage.

Another way of squeezing out more growing space is to cram in more plants than you normally would. In the vegetable plot you can plant in blocks in deep beds rather in rows, which will allow you to grow more plants. Intercrop (plant in gaps) wherever possible. You can also plant more ornamental plants by placing them closer together, but this generally means that you will need to spend more time looking after them. Close planting involves more watering and feeding, or the plants will starve, and it also means keeping a keener eye out for pests and diseases, which are more likely to be a problem in crowded conditions. With care and attention, however, it is surprising how many plants you can get into a tiny space.

An obvious way of growing more plants that is often overlooked is to grow smaller plants. It is amazing how many rock plants, for example you can grow in a trough or old sink.

Create several miniature gardens within your main garden. Small plants can also be grown in pots and arranged on tiered shelves so that they all get plenty of light. Another way is to attach a number of pots or hanging baskets to a pole. You can become absorbed in miniature gardening as there are so many different types of plants that can be grown in this way. One of the real specialist arts, of course, is bonsai.

VISUAL SIZE

Frequently one has contradictory feelings about the size of a garden. Often the intimate atmosphere of a small garden is appealing, but at the same time there is a hankering for it to look bigger. The simplest way of overcoming this dilemma is to disguise the boundaries by covering them with vegetation so that they cannot be seen. This gives the impression that the edge of the garden could be far away, in the unseen distance. This feeling can be enhanced with meandering paths, which vanish out of sight. Unlike a path that can be seen abruptly ending against a fence or a wall, one that disappears around a corner engenders a sense of mystery and uncertainty.

Another way of creating doubt in the mind as to the real boundaries of a garden is by illusion. The simplest way is to use mirrors. Place a mirror on a wall, disguise its edges so that it cannot be perceived to be a mirror and it will give the impression that the garden goes on beyond it.

An alternative method is through the use of paint. A trompe-l'oeil scene on a wall can be deceptive. Even a naïve, romantic scene, which will fool nobody who sees it close to, can have the desired effect of making the garden look bigger when it is viewed from a distance, but a realistic painting can make it appear that the garden does continue on the far side of a painted arch or doorway.

VISUAL ILLUSIONS – MIRRORS

Mirrors are the greatest illusionists of all. In the bathroom they may tell the truth, especially first thing in the morning, but in the garden their role is to fool people into believing that the plot is bigger than it really is.

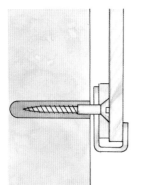

Mirror plates can be used to fix a mirror to a wall without the screw showing. The bottom one is fixed while the top one slides down into position holding the mirror fast.

FIXING A MIRROR

A mirror must be firmly fixed to a wall or fence. It should be made of thick glass and have a waterproof silver backing. A mirror used outdoors will not last forever because the backing eventually breaks down, but its life will be extended if water can be prevented from getting down the back. Cementing it to a wall is one solution, but this creates problems in future years should it be necessary to remove it. It will also cause the mirror to crack if the wall moves or sinks. Special mirror plates, available from hardware stores, are a better option. The edges can be sealed with a mastic filler, similar to the material that is used around baths, or the mirror can be fitted into a frame, which, in turn, can be screwed to a wall.

A mirror fixed to a wall will simply reflect what is in front of it, giving the appearance that it continues behind the wall. If the mirror can be clearly seen to be a mirror the illusion is ruined and the reflection is seen for what it is. If the mirror is disguised, however, by growing vegetation around its edges, for example, it may be so unexpected that the image it reflects truly appears to come from behind, thereby making the garden look bigger.

positioning the mirror

The mirror must be placed in such a way that it reflects something worth showing. It should preferably be set so that it is at an oblique angle to the viewer so that their image is not portrayed and the illusion ruined. The image that the viewer should see is the reverse of the one in front of them. Thus, unless it is identical to what the viewer is looking at, it could be so unfamiliar that they will be fooled into thinking that it is a completely different scene.

To achieve this, therefore, try to have a largish bush or shrub between the viewer and the mirror, with something beyond it – behind it, from where the viewer is standing – that cannot be seen except in the reflection. Even if it is the same scene, the different angle of the reflection is usually sufficient to fool the eye into thinking that it is different. Pathways or paved areas that appear to go on beyond the mirror can be effective in reinforcing the illusion.

framing

Unless the garden is a modern one, where the presence of a mirror can be accepted at face value, it is much better to disguise it, so that the viewer will be unaware that it is there and will not be expecting a reflected scene. The simplest way is to grow a climber or some other vegetation around it, so that the edges are covered and any straight lines, which might give away its presence, are disguised.

Another possibility is to put a trellis framework or doorway around it so that it seems to be an entrance to another part of the garden.

all that glitters

As well as creating illusions, mirrors have another function in the garden – that of creating reflections of light. Fragments can be used in mosaics (see pages 28–9), which may be built into walls or other structures. Small mirrors can be suspended from trees or bushes so that they catch the light as they swing and rotate, and they can be suspended in dark corners so that they catch shafts of light to brighten the gloom.

safety first

While mirrors are extremely effective they can also be dangerous when broken. It is not a good idea to have them in a garden where children play. Elderly and infirm people may also fall against them. So use them with discretion.

A perfect use of a mirror which effectively doubles the size of the pool and the rest of the garden. The mirror is well framed by foliage.

VISUAL ILLUSIONS – *TROMPE-L'OEIL*

If you want a bigger garden, why not just add on a bit next door? There is no need to tell your neighbours. Simply get some extra garden painted on the wall and suddenly your garden has expanded to take in the surrounding countryside.

READY-MADE *TROMPE-L'OEIL*

It is possible to buy ready-made *trompe-l'oeils* in the form of plastic or metal silhouettes, which can be easily fitted to a wall. Choose carefully, because many of these are rather clumsy and do not give the effect they are intended to portray. They can be improved by partially covering them with climbers so that they can be glimpsed rather than seen in totality. These pieces can be simply screwed to the wall: first, drill the holes in the appropriate places and insert plugs before screwing them in place.

The whole purpose of *trompe-l'oeil* is to deceive the eye. Although it is a painting, it is supposed to look as if it is real. An open window, therefore, may be painted on a wall with a scene of, say, a productive vegetable garden glimpsed through it, so that the viewer believes both the window and the scene beyond are real. Close examination will, of course, show that it is not, but that is not the point. At first glance or as a background image, the painting will give the effect it is supposed to and leave you subconsciously thinking that the garden is larger than it is.

subjects

The subject of the picture can be anything you like. If you are simply trying to deceive the casual viewer, perhaps it should be a view of what could be another part of your garden. If, however, you want to impress your visitors, it could be a scene from a much grander garden, such as a vista down an avenue of trees leading to a folly.

If you use plants in the picture, remember that they would, if real, change with the seasons. If you want to do something realistic, it must include plants that are evergreen and change little over the seasons.

You are not restricted to plant themes, of course. The painting could be of a summerhouse or other structure that you would like to build in that position but are, for reasons of space, unable to do so. It can, of course, be treated simply as a piece of decorative art and the subject not necessarily connected with the garden or gardening. In addition to pushing back the boundaries of your garden, *trompe-l'oeil* can be used for other special purposes, including acting as a backdrop. If, for example, you want a yew hedge to back a herbaceous border but have not got a chance of growing one (because there is actually a wall behind the border), you could paint one instead. Many other types of background may seem appropriate, and they can be used three dimensionally – for example, you could paint a mural and stand a piece of sculpture or an urn in front of it.

get out the brushes

The real problem with *trompe-l'oeil* is that although most of us can plant a shrub, few of us are capable of painting a convincing picture. There are only two solutions to this: to commission somebody to paint something for you or have a go yourself and see what happens – at least it should be fun. Commissioning a professional can be expensive, but with the right choice of artist you will be sure of getting something that you will not only enjoy but be proud of owning.

If you decide to do it yourself the easiest way is to copy an existing picture. Draw a grid over the picture and an enlarged grid on the wall. Copy the picture first in pencil and then paint it on the wall. Stick to simple pictures with bold images and colours, which should not be too difficult to copy. Avoid people and animals.

surface

It is possible to paint onto a wooden panel and fix this to the wall. This has the advantages that you can work on it where you like and that you can take it with you if you move house. If you prefer, however, you can paint directly onto the wall or fence, although if the picture is to be realistic the surface should be smooth. The

A *trompe-l'oeil* painted against a wall of a house. Such illusions are particularly useful where it is impossible to grow plants.

area to be painted may need to be plastered before you start. Although it seems obvious, it must be stated that it is essential to use waterproof paints.

getting away from it

As well as creating the illusion of space, *trompe-l'oeil* can be used to create the illusion of place. A rural scene with cows grazing calmly in the fields with hills in the distance can all be viewed through a painted window in the wall, which in reality hides your neighbour, the back of a garage or the street wall. It allows you to place your garden where you want it to be.

VISUAL ILLUSIONS – UNSEEN BOUNDARIES

Boundaries are what determine the physical extent of the garden, the points at which it must end before you start to enter somebody else's territory. One way to deny their presence is to hide them – if you cannot see them, they are not there.

If the margins of the garden are disguised the boundaries will not be seen. Covering them with plants is the most obvious solution. Hedges are the usual boundary vegetation, but they are regular and tend to look like a boundary. If, however, you plant a range of different plants each with a different shape and size the linear quality disappears and what is, in effect, a hedge, appears to be a shrubbery. If there is space these 'hedges' can be more than one plant deep, creating an irregular appearance. False paths can be made through the vegetation, disappearing around a corner before they reach the real boundary, to give the illusion that the shrubbery is densely planted.

Any plants will do in this situation. Shrubs have a more permanent structure than hardy perennials, although they can be mixed. If you want the illusion to remain throughout the seasons, use evergreens, or leaf fall may give the game away.

borrowing space

When you are designing a small garden, one of the tricks you can use to make it appear larger is to 'borrow' features, especially trees, from other gardens. If there is a tall, decorative tree in a neighbouring garden it can be made to appear as part of your own garden as long as the boundary between you and it cannot be seen. Planting shrubs or other plants in front of a fence or wall, for example, so that the boundary is covered but the tree can still be seen peering over the top of the shrubs will make it appear to be part of your garden. By implication, your own garden will seem to be bigger.

sculpting the boundary

It is always a pleasure to discover small, intimate spaces in a garden where you can be private. One way to achieve this is to create an arbour (see pages 106–7). If you are creating a boundary that is thick with bushes and other vegetation, it may be possible to make one or more of these hideaways, simply by growing climbers over a frame or by making 'rooms' in the shrubs, but remember to leave a thick layer between you and the boundary. They will be away from the main part of your own garden, where most activity is likely to take place.

doing away with boundaries

Not all small gardens are found in the centre of towns and cities, surrounded by other houses, of course. Many small gardens are in rural areas or in areas that verge on the country. In these gardens it can be a good idea to open up your own boundaries so that you can see the landscape beyond. Bring it into your own garden and make your plot seem bigger.

One of the more successful ways of doing this is to open only part of the view, rather than all of it, so that occasional glimpses are possible. The classic way to do this is to create a ha-ha, in which the hedge or fence is sunk into a ditch so that it is out of view but still forms a barrier. It makes it look as if the garden continues straight out into the landscape. Building a ha-ha is normally beyond the means of a small garden, but somebody with ingenuity could possibly achieve it, or a version of it, to great effect.

Opposite: A path disappearing into vegetation gives the impression that it continues around the corner and creates the illusion that the garden is bigger than it really is.

VERTICAL SPACE – HOUSE WALLS

If you are interested in growing plants but have only a limited amount of space every scrap must be used. Vertical space, becomes particularly valuable under these circumstances, and one of the most obvious places is the walls of the house.

There is a wide range of climbers and wall shrubs that will happily use the space provided by a wall. Many will easily climb to the eaves; others are shorter and more suitable for growing under windows or against low walls. Some may have a relatively short flowering season, while others, such as some of the modern roses, continue to bloom over a long period. It is possible to grow two climbers, with different flowering seasons, so that they clamber through one another and provide a long season of flowers.

Climbers with fragrant flowers, such as some of the roses, honeysuckles (*Lonicera*) and jasmines, make good plants to grow up house walls. They should be positioned so that their fragrance wafts in through open windows.

covering power

If you are simply using the plants to cover an ugly wall or building, foliage plants are likely to be the best choice, as these have a denser covering power than those grown for their flowers. Evergreen plants, such as ivy (*Hedera*), give the best year-round cover. On the other hand, although they lose their leaves in autumn, many of the deciduous ones, such as Virginia creeper (*Parthenocissus quinquefolia*) or Boston ivy (*P. tricuspidata*), form a dense pattern of branches and shoots, which is enough in itself to provide interest in winter, and the autumn colour, just before the leaves fall, can be superb.

planting

Dig the soil where the climber is to be planted and incorporate as much well-rotted organic material, such as garden compost, as you can. The planting hole should be at least 30cm (12in) from the base of the wall. Plant at the same depth as the plant was in the pot and use a cane or canes to train it towards the wall and the supports.

Most climbers, apart from those that have clinging aerial roots, such as the ivies, need some form of support. The least obtrusive method is to attach horizontal wires across the wall. It is possible to use wooden or plastic trellis, but the wood looks too heavy and tends to dominate the wall, and trellis should be used for small areas rather than over the whole wall. Plastic always looks like plastic, and it breaks down after a bit and is likely to give way suddenly in the middle of a storm.

containers

You may have problems if the area immediately below the wall against which you want to grow climbers is paved. It might be possible to lift a paving slab or a few bricks and plant in the soil revealed. A better option might be to plant the climber in a container, which should be as large as possible to give plenty of root space. It is essential not to let the container dry out, and it is likely to need watering on most days that it does not rain.

FRAGRANT WALL CLIMBERS
Actinidia kolomikta
Akebia quinata (chocolate vine)
Azara microphylla
Itea ilicifolia
Jasminum officinalis (common jasmine)
Lathyrus odoratus (sweet pea)
Lonicera spp. (honeysuckle)
Magnolia grandiflora
Osmanthus delavayi
Trachelospermum asiaticum
Wisteria sinensis (Chinese wisteria)

Climbing plants create a
wonderful colourful effect
when grown up the walls
of a house.

Drill a hole in the wall and
plug it. Screw in a screw eye.

2

Pull the wire through the eye
and twist it securely back on
itself. Continue along the wall.

As the plants grow, tie in the
shoots using string or plastic
plant ties.

ERECTING WIRES

Drill the wall at 1.2m (4ft) intervals, plug the holes and
insert a vine eye in each hole. Thread galvanized wire
through these and secure it at the ends. The wires
should be spaced at 45cm (18in) intervals over the face
of the wall. Plant the plants at least 30cm (12in) away
from the wall and water well. The plants are tied in to
the wires as they grow, using string or plant ties.
Spread out the young shoots at the base of the wall so
that they cover as much of it as possible. Keep the
plants tied in and prune in accordance with the type of
plant used.

VERTICAL SPACE –
ARCHES AND POLES

Any garden that just grows on the flat is, well, boring. Moving up into the air provides a third dimension, which adds greatly to the interest. It also allows for a greater range of plants that can be grown.

The importance of the third dimension, height, in garden design can never be emphasized enough. It is vital in order to achieve structure. Without it, the eye can quickly sweep around the garden and take it all in in one glance. With it, the eye is interrupted, things are hidden and must be sought out. It provides colours, shapes and textures at varying levels and introduces shadow. It also allows various structures to be used and clad in vegetation. Overall, the garden becomes a much more interesting place.

arches

Barriers in the form of fences, hedges or screens divide one part of the garden from another, often making one invisible to the other. An archway is the link, both physically and visually, between the two areas, and it will tend to draw the eye and make visitors to the garden wonder what lies beyond, inviting them to step through. An arch will help to make a small garden far more intriguing and interesting than a completely open one.

Archways can be made from metal or wood, and they can be left unclothed or clad in climbing plants. In most gardens, especially small ones, the latter is preferable. A wide range of climbers will be suitable, but roses are often regarded as the ideal. Always make sure that the arch is going to be wide enough to allow you and, perhaps, your lawnmower to pass through it once it is covered with plants. Having too narrow an arch will be made much worse if the plants in question happen to be prickly roses. Even on arches that are wide enough, it is still a good idea to use a thornless variety such as *Rosa* 'Zéphirine Drouhin'.

hedge arches

Attractive archways can be constructed out of hedging. These are usually more simple to look at because it is not practical to grow climbers over them. Allow the hedge on either side of the entrance to grow up until it is tall enough to pull over to form the arch. A metal former can be used within the hedge, or the branches can simply be pulled over and tied together. Eventually they will fill out, and the arch will simply look like a hole in the hedge.

poles

Arches generally have a purpose in that they are usually the entrance or exit through a hedge or fence, but they are sometimes erected in the middle of nowhere simply as a support for climbers. This can look rather odd. A better idea is to use a simple pole or a series of poles to provide the vertical emphasis. Make certain that each pole is firmly embedded in the ground. For self-clinging climbers, such as clematis, it helps to wrap and staple wire-netting around the pole to give them something to hang on to. Poles are often placed in borders, but they can be used anywhere you want a vertical planting, such as along a path or walk way, where they will provide a rhythmic design. They can be linked with swags of rope, along which the climbers crawl until they eventually merge. Arches can be used in the same way, with a series positioned along a path, and if these are linked in some way they will form a pergola.

Above: Wooden pyramids, tripods or even simple poles, can be used to create vertical planting space in a border.

Opposite, below: A level garden has been made more interesting by the use of raised areas and vertical structures, as well as trees and shrubs.

1	2	3	4	5
Dig a hole at least 45cm (18in) deep where the post will stand.	Use temporary braces to hold the post vertically. Check with a spirit level.	Pack rubble around the post, ensuring that it stays in a vertical position.	Top up the final 15cm (6in) with concrete, sloping the top away from the post.	Plant a short distance from the post and train the plant up a cane towards the post.

   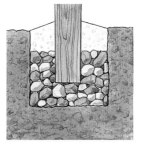 

ERECTING AN ARCH

An arch must be able to withstand a lot of pressure from the wind, especially when it is covered with a leafy climber, and so it must be firmly implanted in the ground. The uprights should be embedded in the ground to a depth of at least 45cm (18in), and they should preferably be concreted in, especially if the arch is in an exposed position. Dig the area where the climbers will be planted and add plenty of well-rotted organic material. Dig a hole and set the plants at the same depth as they were in their pot. Tie them in to the frame of the arch, spreading them out so that they make an effective cover.

CLIMBERS FOR ARCHES

Akebia quinata (chocolate vine)
Campsis radicans (common trumpet creeper)
Clematis spp.
Phaseolus spp. (climbing bean)
Humulus spp. (hop)
Lonicera spp. (honeysuckle)
Rosa spp. (rose)
Vitis spp. (vine)

WORKING IN MINIATURE

One way that a keen plantsperson can grow a lot of plants in a small area is simply to grow small plants. Moreover, since these types of plants can be easily grown in raised beds, they are ideal for people who are unable to tend to conventional ground-level beds.

There is really no limit on the size of a garden: it can consist of a single flowerpot or stretch over hundreds of acres. It is possible to create a garden on a patio, balcony, windowsill or rooftop, and gardeners are not restricted to having large beds filled with soil in which to grow plants. Generally, when one thinks of these areas one thinks of single or limited groups of plants in containers, but there is no reason why, using small plants, a whole garden cannot be created in miniature, including landscaping.

There are two types of small plants to grow – alpine plants and small plants – and they are not necessarily the same. Growing alpines is a specialist art. Some plants are easy to grow, but others, especially the so-called high alpines, are extremely difficult and need a great deal of skill and dedication. One of the secrets of growing good alpines is to use a free-draining but moisture-retentive soil or compost. The actual mixture varies according to the plants grown and the individual grower's preferences, but as with any specialist subject there are plenty of books to consult. Alpine growers tend to be addicted to their craft and spend a great deal of time tending their plants and making field trips to see how they grow in the wild. Once you are bitten with the bug, it can be a fascinating form of gardening, but to do it well you need time and dedication. However, what you don't necessarily need is space, so it is an ideal form of gardening for the owner of a small garden.

small plants

If you do not feel that alpines are for you, there is a wealth of small plants that are not necessarily alpine but that are easy to grow and are ideal for creating a miniature garden. These plants or their seed are readily available and can be used to make a small version of a conventional garden without anything like the amount of labour or effort involved in gardening with alpines. This makes them ideal for the elderly or infirm.

Miniature gardens can be created in conventional beds, raised beds or in a variety of containers. Small pieces of rock can be used to help build up the landscape and small sunken dishes of water can be used to represent ponds. The scale can vary from reasonably sized beds, perhaps several metres (yards) across, to ones built in old sinks or troughs. You could even make a really tiny one in a dinner plate. Inverted dustbin lids and hubcaps from motorcars make good containers. Garden soil can be used in larger beds, but smaller containers should be filled with a general potting compost.

The good thing about such small containers is that they can be placed on tables or raised on piers of bricks so that they are easily accessible to those who have difficulty bending or are confined to wheelchairs. People who may have had to give up conventional gardening but are as keen as ever on growing things have a great opportunity without too much effort.

PLANTS FOR SMALL-SCALE GARDENS

In addition to the many low-growing saxifrages, sedums (stonecrops), sempervivums (houseleeks) and thymes, and smaller bulbs such as crocuses and reticulate irises, the following are suitable for gardening in miniature.

Aethionema spp. (stone cress)
Androsace sarmentosa (rock jasmine)
Aubrieta x cultorum
Campanula cochleariifolia (fairies' thimbles)
Cyclamen spp.
Dianthus 'Inshriach Dazzler'
Erinus alpinus (fairy foxglove)
Erodium reichardii (stork's bill)
Gentiana verna (spring gentian)
Juniperus communis 'Compressa'
Linaria alpina (alpine toadflax)
Polygala chamaebuxus (milkwort)

Rock gardens should look as natural as possible. Here tiny plants nestle in the crevices between rocks.

BUILDING A ROCK GARDEN

Always use local rock if you can – it will look more natural – and do not use rock that is too heavy to move and take care when you are lifting and moving it. It is vital that the soil is free draining. To achieve this, add one part of gravel or grit to two parts of soil and mix. Try to create a natural-looking outcrop with the stone in bands and all sloping back into the soil at the same angle. Pile some soil on the area to be used, which should have first been cleared of all perennial weeds and dug over. Place the first layer of rocks in position, burying at least one-third of the bulk of each rock in the soil. Fill in behind the rocks with soil before adding another tier of rocks. Fill in again and add rocks to cap it off. Plant in the crevices between the rocks and on the ledges. When it is completely planted, cover all visible soil with a layer of gravel or small stone chippings.

BONSAI

Another popular form of miniature gardening is bonsai. As with growing alpines, there are those who become great specialists in the art and even become obsessed with it. It is, however, possible to practise it at a much more humble level and still get a great deal of pleasure and satisfaction from it. Basically, it involves the dwarfing of shrubs and trees, mainly through the careful pruning of shoots and roots, so that the plants grow in small containers. It was originally developed by the Chinese and later adopted and perfected by the Japanese. The techniques are not complicated, but to achieve good results it is essential to follow traditional methods as described in specialist books.

STORAGE IDEAS

One problem with a small garden is that as soon as you start to do anything, whether it is gardening or entertaining, you need somewhere to put things. This takes up space and so you have even less space to do whatever it is you want to do. It can become a vicious circle, so it is important to make the best use of all available storage space.

Below: A small shed hidden behinds shrubs and climbers. Next to it is a discreet compost bin. Both are perfect for a small garden.

Opposite, below: A miniature greenhouse fixed to a wall. Only a small amount of space is needed to grow a surprising number of plants.

If space is severely limited, it is important to think through what you want from your garden and how you can achieve your aims without the problem of storage. If you have a lawn you will need a lawnmower, and you will need a shed in which to keep it. It is possible that you would be better off with a hard surface rather than grass so that you do not have to mow at all. Perhaps the garden furniture should fold flat so that it can be hung on the walls of the garage out of the way of the car, or perhaps it should be durable enough to stand outside all year. If you have a fence rather than a hedge, you do not have to store a hedge trimmer. Think carefully before losing space to storage: do you really need it?

bunkers

Although sheds are the ideal form of storage for almost everything connected with the garden, bunkers or large boxes will take up less space and may provide enough space for the few tools that you need in the garden. As long as it is not too heavy to lift, a mower can also be stored in it. Old coal bunkers are ideal. They could also be built into other features. For example, if you want a permanent barbecue with a built-in sitting area, the seats could be constructed as lockers, with storage space beneath them. Building a wooden deck instead of a patio might allow you to create storage space below it.

camouflage

If your objection to a shed is not so much the space it takes up but its dominant presence, which makes it appear to be too large for the garden, think about disguising it. Painting it green will help to make it merge into the background, and covering it with climbing plants will make it even less noticeable. The plants will soften the edges and break up its surface. If there is space, placing a trellis in front of it, again, possibly covered in climbers, will help to hide it.

changing use

If you have young children, their use of the garden is likely to dominate the layout until they have grown up. Thinking about the long term can make the transition easier, however: a playhouse could be used later for storage purposes and could be positioned, designed and constructed or purchased with that in mind.

greenhouses

Most gardeners hanker after a greenhouse in which to raise a variety of plants. Greenhouses are not only expensive, however, but take up quite a bit of space, especially as the rule of thumb for buying one is that you work out the size you need and double it, because you will always need more space than you think. Although it does not have quite the same prestige as a greenhouse, a cold frame can do almost anything a greenhouse can do, apart from keeping the gardener dry in wet weather. It takes up far less space and can be more easily and cheaply made by the gardener than a greenhouse can.

1 Build a brick structure with three walls and roof it with paving slabs. Put another course of bricks round the top to create a bed.

2 Screw vertical battens on either side of the opening and then attach trellis doors.

3 Once completed, the doors hide the dustbins and the plants disguise the structure.

1

2

3

INCONSPICUOUS SHEDS

In a little garden a small lean-to tool shed can be built against a wall or against a fence if it is substantial enough. (If it is your neighbour's fence you should ask for permission.) This can be big enough to contain the mower and a few tools but will take up little room. A simple frame of 7.5 x 5cm (3 x 2in) timber can be constructed. The sides and the door can be made either by cladding this with feather-edged boarding or by buying some fence panels and cutting them to size. The door can be made in a similar way but will need a 5 x 2.5cm (2 x 1in) frame around the edge to strengthen it. A simple sloping roof can be made from a sheet of cheap plywood covered with roofing felt. Where the top of the roof meets the wall or fence, fill the gap with a flexible filler so that rainwater cannot trickle into the shed. Surround the shed with shrubs so that it cannot be seen.

CONTAINER CULTURE

One of the great things about containers is that they make gardening flexible. This is partly, of course, because the containers can be moved around, making it possible to vary plant combinations and positions. It is also, however, because the choice of containers themselves is so wide. There is a huge variety of standard pots available from garden centres and nurseries, but it is much more exciting to look out for less conventional containers.

There is really scarcely any limit to what can be used, as long as it can hold compost. Some containers that were only recently regarded as unconventional have become almost everyday suggestions as ideas have gained wider acceptance through being shown in magazines and books. Galvanized watering cans, for example, are now quite a common sight. They have the advantage that they fit naturally into the garden scene, as do old buckets, mop buckets, water butts, zinc baths and even old wheelbarrows – all good ideas, and none the worse for being frequently seen. Chimney pots, too, are also popular and suit a variety of plants.

Keen gardeners, however, will keep their eyes open for something that is out of the ordinary. A good source of ideas are junk shops, antique shops, car-boot sales and the like, and these will offer a wide range of objects that are suitable for containing plants. Although many of the best containers have an antique quality about them, for small plants that need little soil, such as sedums (stonecrops), old car hubcaps with holes drilled in them for drainage make good containers.

ADAPTING A CONTAINER

The principles for adapting a container to hold plants are the same no matter what object is selected. For most plants the container should be deep enough for the roots to grow – that is, at least 15cm (6in) deep – although there are a few plants, such as sedums and sempervivums (houseleeks), that will grow in only thin layers of compost, and for these something shallow like a dustbin lid will suffice.

In addition to the container, you will need something with which to make holes in the base, a few stones, potting compost and some gravel or stone chippings for a top-dressing. Before you do anything else, make some drainage holes in the bottom of the container. If the bottom is not flat, the holes should be at the lowest points. Cover the base of the pot with a layer of small stones to improve drainage and fill it with good-quality, general-purpose compost. Add the plant of your choice and top-dress with gravel to add the finishing touch.

If the container is rather plain, decorate it before you fill it by either painting it or sticking objects on the sides. Even conventional flowerpots can be decorated to make them more interesting or more personal. Ordinary terracotta flowerpots can, for example, be painted a different colour. You might choose a single, overall colour or prefer to decorate it with patterns. Be careful to choose a weatherproof paint.

Another way to make containers more personal is to add mosaic or three-dimensional decorations. Shells are a traditional ornamentation, but they can look rather dated unless they are applied with care. You can use pebbles, stones or pieces of wood – almost anything, in fact. It is possible to build up the ornamentation to such an extent that the pot itself is entirely hidden, thereby creating a completely different object, even a piece of sculpture, although still retaining the original pot inside, ready to take the compost and the plant.

A simple solution is to place plain pots inside something else. A wicker shopping basket, for example, can contain several pots, the picture constantly changing as some are replaced when their plants go out of flower.

PUTTING PLANTS FIRST

The line between wit and gimmickry is narrow, and what may seem a good idea can turn out badly. Whatever you choose, remember the dignity of the plants. Do not select a container that belittles the plants or makes them look silly. The plant and its container should enhance each other and look as if they are a whole.

ATTRACTIVE POTS – CONVENTIONAL CONTAINERS

There is a greater range than ever of pots and containers that can be found for sale. They vary in style from the classic to the ethnic and include traditional types, such as barrels. There has also been an extension in the colours available, from earth-coloured ones to shades that will suit any design.

No matter what material or style of container you select, it is important that the pot has at least one drainage hole in the base so that water can drain freely away. Stagnant water spells death to most plants. Placing a layer of broken crocks or tiles or small stones in the bottom of the container will also help with the drainage.

terracotta

Terracotta pots have long been the favourite of most gardeners. It is a sympathetic material that fits in well with both the garden and the plants it contains. Plants also grow well in it. It is porous and so it is difficult to overwater plants (a frequent cause of death), and it is cool in summer and warm in winter. Some terracotta pots are not frostproof and can shatter in a cold winter; these should be placed under cover in very cold weather.

cement and stone substitute

Stone containers are still available but are generally expensive. A great deal of the reproduction ones, which are made of cement or stone substitute, are good imitations and worth buying. Choose with care, however, because the cheaper versions are poor quality even though they, too, will eventually weather and begin to look more attractive.

Containers that are made of cement will also eventually age, although perhaps not as gracefully as stone. If you would like to make a cement container age more quickly, painting it with sour milk will allow spores of lichen and algae to stick to the surface and provide nourishment for them to develop.

ceramics

Until recently terracotta was the only form of ceramic material widely used for garden containers, and because it was unglazed the only available colour was reddish-brown. Now a whole new range of ceramic containers has appeared on the market. Most of these are glazed in a variety of colours and carry a range of incised or slip decorative patterns. Green, blue and brown glazes are among the most popular, but other colours can also be found – in fact, the range is now so wide that it can be difficult to choose.

plastic

Most plastic pots look what they are – plastic – and they do not, on the whole, blend sympathetically in an attractive garden. The recent trend towards glass-fibre reproduction containers has, however, made available a range of pots that are so like the originals that it is difficult to tell them apart without touching them. They include things like lead tanks as well as wine jars and other ancient terracotta containers. They can be expensive. Plastic has one great advantage over other materials in that it is light, which makes it easier to move containers from one place to another, even when they are full of compost. One disadvantage they have is that the sides are not porous and it is easy to overwater.

ANNUALS AND TENDER PERENNIALS FOR CONTAINERS

Argyranthemum frutescens
Begonia semperflorens Cultorum Group
Bidens ferulifolia
Brachyscome iberidifolia (Swan river daisy)
Helichrysum petiolare
Impatiens walleriana (busy Lizzie)
Pelargonium x *hortorum*
Petunia x *hybrida*
Verbena x *hybrida*
Viola x *wittrockiana* (pansy)

Below, left: Large urns and jars
make wonderful containers for
any size of garden. They are
decorative in their own right,
even without their contents.

Below, right: Large pots become
permanent features of a garden
and are big enough to contain
a wide range of plants. They
quickly take on a patina of age.

shapes

As with materials, there has been an explosion in the number of different shapes
and sizes in which pots are available. The basic shape of the everyday flowerpot
still takes a lot of beating for its simplicity, and many plants, such as pelargoni-
ums, are displayed perfectly in them. A row sitting on a wall or windowsill can look
fantastic. Many of the other shapes are derived from classic styles, particularly the
larger urns, but the influx of new glazed ceramics has introduced a whole new
range of shapes.

FREE EXPRESSION – UNUSUAL AND ADAPTED CONTAINERS

There was a time when people used non-conventional containers simply to save money; now they are more frequently used because they can have a quality or character that makes them worth using. After all, you are creating your own garden so why not create your own containers, too?

PAINTING A POT

Clean the surface of the pot thoroughly, especially if it is greasy. Unless you want the natural colour to show through, give the pot a coat of white undercoat. Use masking tape to provide temporary protection for areas that you want to leave their natural colour. Paint the decorations on the undercoat, using gouache paint or, for some less usual shades, tester pots of emulsion paint. When the paint is dry, remove any masking tape and cover the decoration with a layer of matt polyurethane varnish to protect the surface.

PERENNIALS FOR CONTAINERS

Acanthus mollis (bear's breeches)
Agapanthus campanulatus (African blue lily)
Dianthus 'Doris'
Diascia vigilis
Euphorbia characias subsp. *wulfenii* (spurge)
Hosta 'Gold Standard'
Nepeta x *faassenii* (catmint)
Phormium tenax (New Zealand flax)
Primula vulgaris (primrose)
Stachys byzantina (lamb's ears)

Anything that can hold some compost can be used as a plant container. The scope for invention is almost limitless. The object can be used as it is found or it can be fabricated. A simple example of the latter would be to crumple up a piece of thin sheet metal and place the plant within that. Old garden equipment, such as wheelbarrows or watering cans that are no longer required for their original purpose, can be pressed into secondary use as containers, and such objects look natural in the garden and blend in easily.

There are plenty of objects that will make amusing containers – clothing, for example. A pair of old walking boots or wellington boots, filled with compost and planted, are witty objects and at the same time fit into a garden context. You might even consider planting up the pockets of an old raincoat hanging from a nail on the wall or using an old hat as a home for a plant. These items will not last long before rotting or falling to pieces, but that is the point: you do not want them to hang around for ever or the fun will go out of them and they will become boring.

Old toilets have been used as containers, but they must be carefully positioned. Suddenly coming across something like that that is tucked away in an odd corner will have more impact than if it is standing in an obvious position where you cannot fail to see it. Again, do not use it for more than a season or two, or everybody will get bored with the joke, especially if they copied the idea the first time they saw it.

The more unusual objects are always effective if they are used with restraint. One toilet filled with plants may be amusing; twenty will be a waste of space, unless they are part of some great overall design.

fitting the object to the plant

Certain types of containers will suit certain types of plants better than others. Plants with long or vigorous roots will do best in deeper containers, for example. A hosta would look good and would thrive in a large cooking pot, whereas the smaller sedums and sempervivums would look more at home creating a miniature landscape in a dustbin lid or even a hubcap from a car.

The plant should also visually go with the container. Hostas will generally go better with more sober containers, such as the cooking pot suggested above, but brightly coloured annuals look great in a wide range of shapes and objects. Dwarf, bright blue cornflowers, for example, in a tin can suspended from its still-attached lid will look gay and festive, almost like a bunch of flowers thrust into a pot.

Treading the line between what is appropriate and what is not is difficult when it comes to unconventional containers. One person can take a few empty tin cans and convert them into a sophisticated, eye-catching display, while someone else, using the same cans, will produce what just looks like a row of empty baked bean cans, with no aesthetic appeal. Be critical of what you do, and if you have any doubts about your creations, discard them, even though you may have spent time and money working on them.

drainage

Remember that whatever you use as a container must have one or more drainage holes in the bottom. Drill these if necessary, preferably at the lowest points of the container so that no standing water remains.

A close-cropped box
(*Buxus*) surmounted by
a 'crown' creates an
unusual container feature.

ON THE MOVE – GROUPING AND MOVING POTS ABOUT

One of the great advantages of gardening with containers is that, as long as they are not too big, they can be moved, allowing you to create ever-changing scenes. You can swap pots around depending on your mood. You can place them in groups, which can be changed regularly, depending, for example, on what is in flower.

There are two main approaches to the mobile garden. The first is to move a set of pots around, changing their positions and regrouping them from time to time. This can be done just as the mood takes you or it can be done in more systematic way. You may, for example, simply feel like a change, or it may be that one or two of the pots are looking better than others and need moving to the fore for a month or two.

A second approach is to keep pots of plants in reserve, in the greenhouse or tucked away at the bottom of a vegetable plot, say, and to move them into position as you require them or as they come into flower. Bulbs, for example, can be left in their pots, tucked out of the way somewhere until they are next coming into flower. If space is limited, you could remove the bulbs and replant the containers with something else, such as summer bedding plants. If you have the space, this technique will enable you always to have attractive displays. There will be never be an 'in between period' when you are waiting for plants to get going.

pot garden

If you have a garden that has been hard landscaped, virtually all your gardening is going to be done in pots. It is surprising what can be grown in them, even vegetables. You can have different groups of pots representing different areas of the garden – a group of pots containing vegetables, cheerful summer bedding, herbs, a few shrubs and even some flowers for cutting.

creating atmosphere

Pots in containers really come into their own when you are entertaining. You can move plants indoors that will enhance the mood you are trying to create: brightly coloured ones for a party or a convivial evening, or softly coloured ones for a more romantic setting. If you have a terrace, you can stand fragrant plants near to where you may be eating during the evening. On a more practical level, you could place pots of herbs, especially mint, near where you are serving drinks or eating for instant garnishes.

weighing in

The larger pots are extremely heavy when they are filled with compost, especially when the compost is wet, and they will be too heavy to move. Use these as permanent fixtures and put them in position before you fill and plant them. Even smaller pots may be better filled *in situ*, especially if they are awkward shapes, which make carrying difficult.

BULBS FOR CONTAINERS

Begonia x *tuberhybrida*
Chionodoxa luciliae (glory of the snow)
Crocus chrysanthus
Cyclamen hederifolium
Galanthus nivalis (common snowdrop)
Hyacinthus orientalis (hyacinth)
Iris reticulata
Muscari armeniacum (grape hyacinth)
Narcissus tazetta (daffodil)
Tulipa kaufmanniana (water-lily tulip)

SHRUBS FOR CONTAINERS

Acer palmatum var. *dissectum* (Japanese maple)
Buxus sempervirens (common box)
Convolvulus cneorum (bindweed)
Cordyline australis (New Zealand cabbage palm)
Fuchsia magellanica
Hydrangea macrophylla (common hydrangea)
Laurus nobilis (sweet bay)
Rhododendron yakushimanum
Skimmia japonica
Yucca gloriosa (Spanish dagger)

A collection of forcing pots. Although of no use for containing plants, they are very decorative in their own right. They show the advantages of varying heights in a composition.

VARYING THE HEIGHT

When you have a collection of pots it is a good idea to vary the level so that the plants form a cohesive group rather than a random selection of containers that look as if they have just been left to fend for themselves. Place tall plants towards the back and mix the foliage and flowering plants so that they make an attractive combination and colours do not clash. Plants at the back that are obscured by the ones in front of them can be brought into view by being raised off the ground. Place the pots on some form of support, such as bricks or upturned pots. If you want them much higher a specially made table or shelf will be needed, but make sure that it is properly made and sturdy.

PILE THEM HIGH – CONTAINERS ABOVE GROUND LEVEL

Many people regard container gardening as nothing more than having a few well-positioned pots on a terrace or beside the front door. Containers can, however, be used to advantage at any height. They can be placed on the tops of walls or on windowsills, or they can be suspended from the branches of trees or even from the eaves. Balconies and rooftops also provide planting places, as long as you are prepared to use containers.

Windowboxes are useful items, which need not be used only on windowsills. Because they are reasonably large you can get quite a number of plants in each one, and this allows you to create a series of miniature gardens, each one as colourful or as subtle as you wish. Such boxes have the advantage that they can be fitted virtually anywhere. Windowsills are the obvious place, of course, although they are better suited to houses with inward-opening or sash windows than those with outward-opening casements. Even if a window opens outwards, however, a box can be fixed to the wall below the window rather than on the window ledge itself.

Windowboxes can also be fixed on blank walls and can do much to cheer up what could otherwise be a rather bleak scene. There are also a large number of containers, mainly ceramic but also of plastic, that have been especially designed for fixing to walls. Many are the equivalent of half a conventional pot, so that it has one flat side instead of being completely round. These are often small enough to hang on a hook or nail.

swinging flower power

Hanging baskets are another way of filling vertical space with plants. Over the years many new varieties of colourful plants have been bred with a trailing habit, and they are ideally suited to these containers. They can be suspended from any overhang or from brackets fixed to vertical walls. They can also be hung from poles placed around the garden, perhaps next to a patio or along a path. These could also support lighting of various sorts.

security

Once you move pots of soil and plants above ground level you immediately have the potential for accidents. It is essential that all containers are well fixed to a wall or other structure. A windowbox may feel quite secure when it is sitting on a windowsill, but a strong wind funnelling off a wall can easily whip it to the ground. Screw or chain everything down.

managing water

The main problem with all pots is watering. Containers usually need to be watered at least once a day and more often than that in hot weather. This is tedious enough on the ground, but once containers are above head height, it gets difficult to lift a watering can sufficiently high to pour out the water. One solution is to use a hosepipe attached to a cane or broomstick that can be easily raised in the air. The other method is to use one of the pump-action watering devices that have a long lance with a bend on the end. Pumping forces the water up and out into the container.

don't forget the roof

Some people, especially those in flats and apartments, have no garden at all. However many do have a balcony or even access to the roof. Both of these make admirable places for creating small potted gardens. Before you begin, make sure that the structure is strong enough to support the extra weight. Roof areas may

Left: Raising a container even a little way off the ground will make all the difference to its appearance by giving it a sense of majesty.

1
Place the hanging basket in a bucket to support it and put the liner in position.

2
Part fill the basket with compost and then push the roots of the side plants through holes in the liner.

3
Continue to fill the basket with compost and then add the remaining plants to the top. Water thoroughly.

FILLING A HANGING BASKET

Stand the basket in a bucket so that the round bottom does not roll around while you are working on it. Add a liner, of which there are several types from which you can choose. Partially fill the basket with a good-quality container compost. Cut up to three slits around the basket, level with the surface of the compost, and poke a plant through each slit. It is best to wash off the compost from the roots of the plant and to wrap the roots in wet paper tissue. Poke this through the slit from the outside, remove the paper and spread out the roots. Continue to fill the basket with compost until it reaches the rim and firm down. Plant the remaining plants in the top of the basket and level off the soil, removing or adding some so that the final surface is just below the rim of the basket. Water thoroughly and hang up.

need adapting, not only to make them capable of bearing the load but also so that there is an acceptable surface for walking on. Flat lead roofs, for example, look ideal but the lead can easily be punctured and will need decking above it. If you are at all unsure, get professional advice. Ordinary sloping roofs can be used as growing areas in their own right. Make up a handful of sticky compost, place it on the roof and plant a small sedum or houseleek (*Sempervivum*) in it. They will spread using dust and detritus as soil.

THE OUTDOOR LIFE

Unless you use your small garden as nothing more than a convenient place to store unwanted items, you are likely to regard it as somewhere you can relax in one way or another. Children find running about and playing games relaxing, and some adults find gardening relaxing, but for most people relaxing in the garden means nothing more than sitting in the sun or shade, reading or dozing or, perhaps slightly more energetically, entertaining in one way or another.

If the garden is going to mean anything at all in your life it must surely become the focus of your periods of relaxation. If a garden is nothing but a chore or a millstone, this is a sign that something is wrong and needs to be put right. Change the layout and the amount of work that is required in its upkeep until you find that you have got more time to relax. This may ultimately mean going to the extreme and covering the space completely with concrete and placing a sun-lounger in the middle. If this improves your quality of life then it is the ideal design for you.

There are many people who find that spending an hour or so weeding or deadheading is both therapeutic and relaxing, but do not feel guilty if you are not among their number. Your garden should reflect your lifestyle, and that goes for the ways you choose to relax. It should not be a status symbol, and it is not the place for 'keeping up with the Joneses' at the expense of having time to enjoy the space.

SITTING AROUND

People probably spend more time sitting around in their gardens than doing anything else, and so it is worth designing or adapting the garden to take this into account. Areas in both sun and shade can be developed so that seats and sun-loungers can be used in comfort without them rocking irritatingly whenever you shift your position. Other areas might be designed to be more private spaces, where you can sit, surrounded by plants in peaceful seclusion, reading or dozing, away from the activities of the other members of your household.

The ultimate way of relaxing for many people is to swing gently to and fro in a hammock, snoozing or reading, a drink within easy reach. For many people this is the lifestyle they would aspire towards, but there is no reason why you could not achieve this in your own garden, provided, of course, that you can find the time to take advantage of your quiet corner.

SHADY BUSINESS

People are becoming increasingly aware of the dangers associated with spending too much time exposed to sunlight. In the past, patios used to be sited so that they were in full sun for the maximum amount of time, but now it is regarded as not only more sensible but also more comfortable to relax in the shade. Some gardens have natural shade in the form of a mature tree, but others need to have some form of shade created. This is not the problem it may seem and need not be unsightly.

EATING OUT

Alfresco eating is becoming increasingly popular, both for family meals and for entertaining guests. This may require nothing more than a simple flat area where a table and chairs can be placed, but as people want increasingly to eat in the shade, away from the burning sun, pergolas, arbours and other shade-producing devices have been constructed to provide a dappled light. In the evening, dining areas complete with soft lighting and fragrant plants provide a romantic, relaxing setting.

COOKING OUT

Although eating out often involves carrying the food that has been cooked in the house or elsewhere to the table set outdoors, the use of barbecues to cook the food right next to where it is to be eaten is increasingly popular. Sometimes all that is needed is a flat surface on which the barbecue can stand, but more and more often specially built structures that are integral parts of the garden are required.

RELAXING –
CONVENTIONAL SEATING

The provision of garden furniture is big business these days, which is good news for gardeners since it gives them a wide choice of options. First-time buyers can purchase something cheap, and later, as more money is available, better built and more luxurious items can be acquired.

When you go to choose chairs it is a good idea to try them out by sitting in them. There is such a wide range available that it makes sense to look at as many as you can and choose the most comfortable that you can find. Sometimes you may have to decide between comfort and appearance, as the two may not go together. If you are going to use them a lot, comfort must play a large part in your decision.

There was a time when all garden furniture seemed to consist of folding, tubular aluminium frames and nylon fabric. Fortunately, styles and materials have moved on a bit. Such chairs are still available, especially second-hand, and they are often inexpensive. Extra cushions will make them more comfortable. They make

Opposite, left: This rustic
arbour and bench, surrounded
by a profusion of golden hops
(*Humulus lupulus*) provide
a tranquil seating area.

Below: A simple garden bench
becomes an eyecatching feature
when painted bright blue.

ideal reserve chairs in case you suddenly have to find space for extra guests, and they can be folded away until required.

As general-purpose garden seats tubular aluminium chairs have been replaced by moulded plastic, which are inexpensive and often surprisingly comfortable. They are tough and durable and can be left outside all year round, although they will last longer and keep their finish better if they are stored away during winter. The non-folding chairs, which are light and easy to move, can be stacked to minimize storage space and can be used either at a table or by themselves. They are usually white, green or brown, and although not particularly attractive, they can even be moved indoors to help seat a large party.

Cane furniture is often relatively cheap and is light for moving about. However, it must be stored when not in use otherwise it will quickly deteriorate.

sitting upright

The variety of wooden seating has increased dramatically in recent years. Some of it is relatively cheap, but at the other end of the scale are some extremely expensive ranges of matching chairs, tables and loungers. Some of the cheaper items look what they are, but price is not necessarily an infallible guide, so rather than buy directly from advertisements, look at what you are going to get for your money, to avoid disappointment. You may be lucky and find a bargain.

Wooden seating varies from individual chairs to benches. The chairs can be upright styles, which are useful at tables as well as by themselves, or they may be reclining chairs of some sort. Many of the hardwoods are tough enough to require no treatment, but some are best given an annual application of preservative or at least a thorough brush down with a wire brush to remove any lichen and algae that might be growing on them, especially if they are in the shade. Always choose furniture that is guaranteed to have been made from wood from a renewable source.

Similar conventional seating is produced in metal. Much of it is cast and has intricate designs and patterns. The alloy ranges are reasonably trouble free, but those made of iron and steel will need to be painted from time to time to prevent them from rusting. Metal is not as comfortable as wood when it used for long periods without some form of padding.

lounging about

As well as conventional upright chairs, benches and reclining chairs, there are several other pieces of furniture aimed specifically at those who want to relax. Sun-loungers, which are, effectively, folding beds, can be used in both the sun and the shade. In the past they have mainly been made of aluminium tubing, but now they are available in plastic as well as wood. Many are quite uncomfortable for lying on without something soft on top of them, but most are available with cushions or thin mattresses.

Really luxurious loungers are hung from frames so that they swing gently when you sit or even lie on them. They usually have a sun shade or canopy incorporated into the framework.

STORING FURNITURE

All forms of furniture benefit from being protected from winter weather. If you have space, the garage or shed is the best place. Alternatively, if furniture can be stacked into a neat pile, it can be wrapped in a polythene cover. Special covers can be purchased for garden furniture, but any tough material will do. Before storing, clean each piece off and, if they are wood, apply a coat of preservative. Check that every piece is dry before storing.

RELAXING – ALTERNATIVE SEATING AND UNUSUAL FURNITURE

Although seating should be designed for comfort, there are a few types that are made and acquired more for their appearance than anything else, although they may be comfortable enough for occasional sitting on. Some are serious seats, others can be just for fun.

tree seats

If you have a large tree in the garden, building a seat around it can make an attractive feature. You can buy custom-built ones, but they may be difficult to find and are likely to be expensive. With a little ingenuity and a few pictures of examples, it should not be too difficult to build one. Remember not to make it too tight to the tree, which must have room to grow. These seats look particularly elegant when they are painted white. Elegant they may be, but they are not sociable, because your companions are likely to be sitting with their backs to you in an outward-looking circle.

fragrant comfort

A development of the turf seat (see opposite) is to construct one with a camomile seat. This will produce a wonderful fragrance when it is sat upon. As with the basic turf seat, build a box of wood or brick, fill it with soil and plant the camomile on top. The plant you need is *Chamaemelum nobile* 'Treneague'. This is a tough, compact form, which does not flower. Plant at 15cm (6in) intervals across the seat, and water regularly until the plants are established. Trim the camomile occasionally to keep it neat. As an alternative, thyme makes a tough and fragrant surface for a seat. Take care that you do not sit on when it is in flower – it is likely to be covered in bees!

a seat from the past

An old-fashioned type of seat, a lovers' seat is a bench that is shaped like a letter S, enabling the occupants to sit side by side but at the same time facing in opposite directions. The indoor equivalents are called tête-à-têtes, and they permit intimate conversation but restrict the action. It is perhaps not a style of seating that would be used a great deal, but it can look decorative, and it is useful to have somewhere in the garden where you can just rest for a few minutes. Not all seating will be sat on for hours on end.

Another kind of seat from the past that is due for revival is a mobile bench. It looks a bit like a cross between a bench and a wheelbarrow, with a wheel at one end, handles at the other and a bench in the centre. The simple idea behind this is that you can move the seat anywhere in the garden you want without having to strain to lift it.

second-hand seats

For casual seating around the garden, quite a number of old seats and garden chairs can be bought at boot fairs and from junk shops. These are becoming more difficult to find as they are increasingly deemed to be antiques rather than jumble, but they do still turn up. They are often in a rather battered state, and you may think that they could be more usefully employed as sculpture in the garden than as seating. You may, however, come across some pieces that can be done up and used, especially as reserve seating for when you have a lot of visitors.

getting down to it

Finally, don't overlook one type of seating that is available to everyone – the ground. A blanket or rug, some cushions and little else is required.

Opposite, below: An ordinary
garden bench has been adapted
to make a chamomile seat that
will give off a delicious scent
when it is sat on.

Below: Tree seats have a long
history and still make an impact
when used today. They can be
purchased ready made or made
to suit the garden.

TURF SEATS

An unusual seat but one that can be enjoyable to both construct and use is a turf seat.
In its most basic form it can simply be a rectangular block of earth covered in turf.
The sides, front and back may need supporting, and these can be made out of planks
of wood, bricks or thin sticks woven between uprights to form a wattle wall around
the seat. The same wattle can be used to create a round seat, which can be positioned
anywhere and is not difficult to dismantle and build somewhere else in the garden
should the need arise. A similar type of seat could be cut into a bank if you have a
sloping or terraced garden.

RELAXING – HANGING ABOUT IN HAMMOCKS

The ultimate way of relaxing in a garden is in a hammock. It somehow seems the height of luxury to many people, even more so than sitting in a comfortable chair or on a lounger. Hammocks are readily available and are not difficult to hang, but it is obviously important to make certain that they are well secured.

INSECT NETS

In areas where insects are likely to be a pest it is a good idea to have some form of protection in the form of a net. This is especially important if you are likely to fall asleep and not be conscious of the pest until it has stung you. A fine net curtain will suffice, provided it is large enough. If you have a hammock that is hung on a frame the net may be built into it, but otherwise it must be hung from a tree or suspended on a line between the two anchor points.

There are plenty of hammocks to choose from, both at garden centres and other shops and through mail order outlets. Many are made from canvas or some other cloth, while others are made from netting. When you buy, it is essential that you get something that is safe and strong enough to take the weight of the heaviest member of the family. Although a hammock is best taken inside when not in use, few people have such well-ordered lives, and the hammock will often be left outside in rain and sun. It is therefore important that it is made of strong material that will not rot. A hammock that suddenly splits can provide an uncomfortable, if not dangerous, experience.

locating and hanging

The best place for a hammock is in a shady spot under a tree, possibly where a light breeze is likely to play so that the hammock is gently rocked. Avoid full sun, because it is only too easy to fall asleep in a hammock and end up being fried.

It is essential to ensure that your hammock is secure. It must have strong supports. The classic position (apart from on board ship) is slung between two trees, and if this is feasible in your garden, go for it, because it is the ideal setting. However, you must practise your knots and make sure that they are secure: a bow-line fits the bill and will not let you down. Most good hammocks are supplied with the means of support and instructions for tying.

Not everyone has convenient trees in their garden, but it is possible to anchor the ends of a hammock to walls or some other structure. These are not always in the right place, however, and the simplest answer may be to buy a special frame, which can be placed anywhere in the garden. These work well and can incorporate a canopy. The only problem is that they do take up a lot of space in a small garden when not being used and that, of course, is most of the time. Fortunately, many of the modern ones either take to pieces or fold up.

luxurious alternatives

Hammocks are not the easiest things to erect and get into. Help is at hand in the form of an alternative if you like the image but find the execution just a bit too difficult or boring. You can buy a swinging lounger that is suspended in a frame but is more like an airborne sofa than a hammock. It is possible to sit as well as lie on this, and several people can use it at the same time, something that can be risky in a proper hammock. These loungers are often referred to as hammocks in catalogues.

Opposite: Hammocks are a classic way of relaxing in the garden. They need strong supports and are best placed in dappled shade.

IN THE SHADE – CREATING COOL RETREATS

In the middle of winter one tends to dream of hot, sunny days, but when they arrive it soon becomes apparent that you can have too much of a good thing and one starts to look around for cool shade. There is nothing quite like relaxing over a meal in the dappled shade in a hot Mediterranean country, so why not create it at home?

MAKING AN AWNING

An awning can be permanently attached to the house or garden wall and pulled out when required, or it can be hung from hooks on one side, with poles on the other. Cut and hem a piece of canvas or other material to the size of awning you want and add eyelets in each corner and in the centres of two opposite sides. At the appropriate height, drill and plug holes in the house wall at the same intervals as the eyelets and insert a cup hook in each. Hang the awning from these. Knock an 8cm (3in) nail in each end of a pole. Place the nail at one end of the pole into an eyelet in the free end of the awning. Pull the awning tight and insert the nail in the other end into the ground or into a joint in the paving slabs. Tie a rope from the top nail back to a peg in the ground to form a guy rope. A more attractive awning can be constructed by sewing a pelmet around the front and side edges. A free-standing awning away from the wall can be made with posts at each corner (plus one in the middle of each side if the awning is large), each of which should have two guy ropes.

Trees undoubtedly give some of the best shade. This is not a problem if you already have trees growing in the garden, but if not you must think about including them in your long-term planning. Many trees are, of course, the wrong shape for sitting under. Tall, thin ones are too narrow to produce adequate shade, while wider ones can be too dense. The ideal shape is a spreading tree that does not have too thick a canopy of branches. You can thin the branches on an existing tree so that the shade is dappled – that is, so that a little sunlight filters through. Old apple trees are ideal for this, but take care that the visual shape of the tree is not ruined.

shady bowers

Another excellent source of shade can be created by constructing a framework over which climbing plants are allowed to grow. The classic Mediterranean plant for this is the grape vine (*Vitis*, see p84), which is ideal because although the individual leaves are quite large there are not enough to provide complete coverage, making the shade dappled. The vines can be varities capable of producing fruit or those that are grown purely for their ornamental leaves. There are plenty of other climbing plants to choose from, including roses and honeysuckle, which add fragrance to the shade.

Construct a sturdy framework of wood treated with preservative, sinking the bases into the ground to a depth of at least 45cm (18in). Plant one climber on three sides of the arbour, leaving the fourth open. This will create a space with an enclosed, intimate feeling. Alternatively, plant on one side only, leaving the other sides open to create a sense of more space, as well as providing a view. A paved area beneath the shade will proved a good, stable surface on which tables and chairs can stand.

temporary shade

Awnings and garden tents are a popular and quick way of creating shade. They have several advantages over natural vegetation, the chief of which is that they can be packed away when they are not in use, allowing light and sun to return to the area. This is particularly valuable in a small garden, where there is not enough room to have both a sunny and a shady sitting area. Another advantage is that you can choose the colour of the fabric, perhaps even having reversible fabric, that has bright, cheerful colours on one side and cool, soft ones on the other. Virtually any fabric can be used, although with more permanent awnings a weatherproof material, such as canvas, should be used. Split-bamboo cane blinds can be used to create excellent dappled shade.

Garden tents are also becoming more widely available. These are usually erected on a simple framework with four poles, a top and a pelmet, but no sides. One or two sides can be attached to keep out wind and even rain.

movable shade

The most versatile shade is that provided by an umbrella or parasol. This has the advantage that it can not only be packed up when not required, but can also be easily moved and erected wherever it is required. The two disadvantages are that many are rather small and there is not enough space for a group of people to sit comfortably under them, and they also need heavy bases to stop them from blowing over.

One way of creating
semi-artificial shade is to
build an arbour and cover it
with climbers to produce a
dappled shade.

ENTERTAINING – DINING

One of the greatest joys of having a garden is being able to eat outside. A meal taken outdoors never seems as rushed as one eaten inside and is a good aid to relaxation. In reality, meals eaten outdoors are not much different from meals eaten indoors, apart, of course, from the location.

One aspect of eating outdoors that is often overlooked but that is essential to enjoyment is a sturdy, stable table. A flimsy one that rocks can be irritating, and it is hardly conducive to a relaxing meal if the table moves a different way every time someone attacks their plate. A level patio or an area of flat lawn is needed to make sure that everything remains on an even keel. Tables that are used outside should be as large as possible, with plenty of space for bowls of food and ample room for several people to sit around them. The chairs, too, should be stable and of a height that is comfortable for eating.

If the food is prepared in the house and brought outside, a position not far from the house is more convenient, otherwise the cook may do a lot of running about. On the other hand, it is sometimes pleasant to get as far away from the house as possible, and an area partly surrounded by shrubs may be more to your liking. If you are having a barbecue, the table should be near the cooking area, although not so close that the diners are enveloped in the smoke and smells.

If you are planning to eat only in the evening, sun and shade are not important considerations, but for daytime occasions it will be necessary to decide where the table should be sited. More and more people are preferring to sit in shade rather than face the risk of being burned by the sun and possibly contracting skin cancer. Some people still prefer the sun, however, especially in cooler areas.

The simplest solution if you want some shade is to eat under a large tree, but not everybody has one in their garden or has a neighbour with a tree that overhangs sufficiently to cast enough shade. You can plant a tree, but it will be many years before it is big enough to shade an entire dinner party. In the meantime, an arbour or a pergola is ideal (see pages 106–7). All that is required is a framework of posts with crossbars attached to the top, over which climbing plants grow, providing the shade. Grape vines (*Vitis*), either productive or ornamental, provide a delightful, soft, dappled light. An alternative is a canvas awning, which will have the advantage of being waterproof in case of a sudden shower (see pages 82–3).

the 'dining room'

Many people feel more comfortable eating in an enclosed space than in the open. Although they do not actually want to be in a room, they prefer to be within an enclosure of some sort. This could be provided by shrubs and trees in a little glade or by an arbour. On the other hand, the skeleton outline of a room, provided by four posts and crossbars, may be sufficient to create the illusion of the space. Such a framework is even better if covered by a creeper to keep out the sun. In the evening such a structure can be used to support lights. Even sitting on a small terrace rather than on an expanse of lawn somehow seems to define space and make people feel more comfortable.

picnicking

Young children often like to do something in imitation of the adult world, and having picnics in the garden is always fun for them, especially if they are in an area that is tucked away out of sight of the house. Somewhere at the bottom of the garden or in a secluded corner, hidden by, or created under, shrubs to make it a secret and private place, is ideal. Perhaps it could double as a 'camp'.

Opposite: An arbour makes an ideal place for dining. The frame creates an exterior dining room.

Below: Dining areas need not be covered. They can be shaded by trees and surrounded by bushes to create a private space.

ENTERTAINING – BARBECUES

Allied to the growth of interest in eating outside is a similar growth in cooking outside – indeed, for many people the opportunity it offers for barbecues is the whole point of having a garden. It is fun, the food tastes different from anything cooked inside, and it is a good way to entertain both family and friends.

Below: There is nothing quite like food cooked and eaten in the open air.

Opposite, above: Barbecues can be free-standing and mobile, or, as here, built in so that they are part of the garden structure.

Visit any large DIY store or garden centre in early summer and you will see a wealth of different styles of barbecue. Some are relatively cheap and basic, while others are expensive and have many sophisticated extras. From the cooking point of view, many people find that the simplest and least expensive models work perfectly well and do exactly what they want. Although they are often left outside all year round, barbecues should be stored away when not in use and will therefore need storage space, which should be a consideration in a small garden.

Just like the free-standing type, built-in barbecues can be as simple or as sophisticated as you wish. The most basic type is little more than a brick hearth, possibly with somewhere to put tools and food, although a table will often serve just as well. If the bricks are not bonded with cement, the barbecue can be taken apart and built somewhere else in the garden, and if paving slabs are used as foundations, the whole thing will be quite mobile. For the true barbecue *aficionado* a properly built structure is more likely to include a whole area devoted to alfresco cooking and eating, with built-in seats, tables and even cupboards, and a barbecue that includes a flue.

Ready-bought barbecues are obviously made from metal, but home-made ones can often be made from scrap materials that may be to hand, such as old bricks or pieces of stone or concrete blocks. If the finished structure looks a bit scrappy and untidy, it could be roughly plastered to give it a Mediterranean or Mexican look.

locating a barbecue

In many ways, a mobile barbecue is best because you have the flexibility to place it in the most suitable position for that particular day. It is the working centre of the party where everything happens, and the cook will want to be as close as possible to the rest of the party. On the other hand, barbecues have the great disadvantage of producing both smoke and cooking smells. These may be tolerable to the participants, even though they probably prefer not to be directly next to them, but remember that your neighbours might find them both a nuisance and an intrusion. So, if possible, place the barbecue where the prevailing wind will blow the smoke and smells where they will not worry anyone. This is more difficult with a built-in barbecue, and if you do build a permanent structure, a chimney will help to funnel the pollutants away. Before you build, try to determine the direction of the prevailing winds.

safety

Barbecues involve fire and this, obviously, can be dangerous. Do not place a barbecue against a wooden fence. Make certain that it is completely stable and that there is no possibility of it falling over. Take special care when there are children in the garden. Leave hot coals to cool before disposing of them.

planting near the barbecue

There should, clearly, be no plants in the immediate vicinity of the barbecue, simply because they are likely to get scorched. You might, however, want to have some herbs planted not too far away so that you can pluck a handful of fresh mint, chives or rosemary without having to walk to the other side of the garden to find them.

1

Make a solid foundation on which to build the barbecue.

2

Build up a square box of bricks and cover it with a paving slab.

3

Continue the wall on three sides to surround the fire and support the grill.

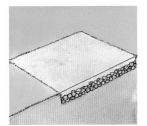
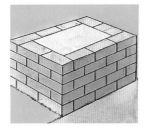
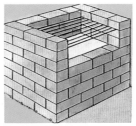

BUILDING A BARBECUE

The simplest form of home-built barbecue can be made from bricks. First, dig foundations by removing 15cm (6in) of soil over the whole area of the base of the barbecue, ramming in 10cm (4in) of hardcore and covering this with 5cm (2in) of concrete. Build a square of bricks up to four or five layers high and then fill the middle with hardcore. Lay a 5cm (2in) layer of concrete on this. Continue to build up the sides and back, leaving the front open. Build in supports, such as lengths of iron bars, for the grill shelf at intervals up the side walls. Leave the cement and concrete to set thoroughly before use.

Pieces of statuary and sculpture in the garden add a pleasing touch, especially when well sited so that the beauty of the piece can be enjoyed.

The main thesis of this book is that a garden, no matter what its size, should be for relaxation. When you are sitting or lying in the garden, the factors that will help you relax relate mainly to the senses: sight, sound, smell and taste. These are key factors in any garden, and any makeover should incorporate them in its design.

SIGHT

The feel of the garden is important. Some are dull and boring, and this will rub off on the inhabitants, making it a dull and boring place to be in and therefore not particularly relaxing. Others are full of vibrancy and excitement, which can be great for parties and other types of entertainment, but not necessarily conducive to relaxation. A romantic aura, on the other hand, created by soft colours and soft outlines, is another matter. The romantic mood can be enhanced in the evening by subtle lighting, carefully located in the garden. Bear in mind that garden lighting can be atmospheric and need not be limited to blazing halogen security lamps, which reveal everything in their harsh glare.

SOUND

The garden can to a certain extent be insulated from surrounding noise by thick vegetation – hedges and shrubs in particular are useful for helping to cut out intrusive noise – but the real benefits come from within the garden itself. Sounds, such as the tinkling of moving and falling water, the rustling of leaves and the singing of the birds, contribute to a general feeling of well-being and total relaxation.

TOUCH

Touch does not play a major role in relaxation as far as the garden is concerned, although it still plays a part. Running your fingers through soft grasses and through the leaves of such tactile plants as rosemary as you walk past is a sensuous and calming experience. Many people derive pleasure from simply sitting on grass, because of its 'feel', which is quite different, for example, from sitting on the paving slabs of a patio.

SMELL

After sight, smell is the most important sense that we use in the garden. Fragrant plants are always a joy, whatever the time of day. In the morning there are fresh, invigorating scents, enhanced by cool air and the dew, while in the drowsy afternoon, with the warmth come the fragrances of various plants. At dusk come the heavily sweet scents of the evening and night. All these contrive to relax us, and in any garden makeover it is essential to include plants that will contribute to the fragrances that only the garden can produce.

TASTE

There is nothing like the taste of fresh vegetables and fruit straight from the garden. It is impossible to buy produce that even approaches the flavour of something picked in the garden. Although the way the plants are grown and the varieties chosen contribute, it is the fact that the time lag between something being picked and eaten is minimal that makes home-produced fruit and vegetables so delicious. In a small garden it is difficult to find space to provide a year-round source of vegetables, but enough can be grown at least to remind you what real food actually tastes like.

SATISFYING THE MIND

Not all relaxation comes from being able to wallow in the comfortable surroundings of your garden. Stimulation of the mind also helps to reinvigorate us for the rigours of another day. One way to do this is to include pleasing objects in the garden – pieces of sculpture or topiary, for instance – that are not only a pleasure to have but may also be a little thought provoking.

ROMANTIC SETTINGS

At the end of a hard day, relaxing in a garden filled with soft colours and imagery is a wonderful way to recharge the batteries. Some gardens are more conducive to this kind of relaxation than others, and choosing the right plants is an important step towards creating the right ambience.

Because plants are so influential when it comes to establishing mood and atmosphere in a garden, selecting the appropriate plants and putting them in the right setting deserves some thought. Of all possible arrangements, a romantic setting is probably the most relaxing.

This will usually involve plenty of vegetation but not much open space. Paths will wind past fragrant bushes and arbours, and places to sit will be cut out of the undergrowth. Climbers, especially roses and honeysuckle, will clamber up through trees and over arches. Borders will have softly coloured plants that go harmoniously together without a hint of clashing shades.

All this can be achieved in a small garden with a little imagination and effort. It depends, first, on getting the structure right and, second, on choosing the right plants. Some gardeners will be able to see in their mind's eye exactly how they can transform their own gardens, but others will need some help.

Look at books and magazines, but, more importantly, visit as many other gardens as you can before you start work. See how other gardeners have coped with similar problems to your own. Even looking at big gardens will help, because they often contain intimate areas and even the juxtaposition of one or two shrubs may trigger ideas.

plants

Choosing the right plants is the key. On the whole bright colours create excitement and are great for party settings, perhaps planted in the neighbourhood of a barbecue, but softer colours are generally more relaxing.

Pastel blues, pinks and yellows go well together. Brighter colours are best planted in drifts, which blend into one another, and mixing them results in a spottiness that becomes restless. Softer colours mix well together, and although drifts still look best, individual plants can be mixed, creating a haze of colour.

single colour

White gardens or even a white border will help create the impression of tranquillity and peace. Although they are called white borders, they always consist of two and sometimes three colours. In addition to the white flowers, there is, of course, green foliage, and there is also grey or silver foliage, which blends in well with this type of border. Any white flowers will do, although avoid using too many creams, or the purity of the colour will not come through.

One advantage of a white border or garden is that the flowers stand out at dusk and can often be seen long after dark, in a ghostly after-image of the border. Other single colours can be used, but they do not have the same qualities as all-white borders. Purple, borders, for example, can be interesting for a while, but unless well thought out, they can become leaden and heavy. Brighter colours such as hot reds or oranges are too exciting for a romantic setting. If well done, pinks or pale blues can help create the right atmosphere.

SWAGS

A neat garden with everything in its place tends to feel a bit like a straightjacket, and most people are more at ease in a garden that is soft around the edges. The beds are informal without being untidy, and trees and shrubs are less like soldiers and more like clouds. Climbers always add interest to the scene and can look wonderfully informal if they are tied up in swags. Roses growing along ropes or enclosing a sitting area in great folds are a delightful way of enhancing a romantic corner. Place 10 x 10cm (4 x 4in) wooden posts in the ground at intervals of about 3m (10ft), concreting them in to make sure that they do not get blown over. Nail a thick rope between the tops of the posts, allowing it to sag slightly in the middle to form a smooth curve. Plant a rose at each post and tie it in. As it grows, tie the stems upwards and eventually along each rope.

A white garden has a peaceful feel about it and is very romantic. Roses are a must in such a situation.

WHITE FLOWERS

Anemone x *hybrida* 'Honorine Jobert'
Aster novae-angliae 'Herbstschnee' ('Autumn Snow')
Camellia 'Swan Lake'
Clematis 'Marie Boisselot'
Dianthus 'Haytor White'
Lamium maculatum 'White Nancy'
Magnolia stellata (star magnolia)
Nicotiana sylvestris (tobacco plant)
Philadelphus 'Sybille'
Rosa 'Iceberg'

RESTFUL SOUNDS

Mention sound to most people in connection with a garden and they immediately think of a neighbour's lawnmower or barking dogs. But there are lots more sounds that can be found in the small garden, many of them pleasant and restful on the ear.

Natural sounds, such as the singing of birds or the humming of bees, are wonderfully therapeutic and are a perfect background to relaxation. Bushes and shrubs are likely to attract birds of many kinds to a garden, and lawns will bring in blackbirds and thrushes. Seedheads on flowers will attract a wide range of birds and insects on plants will attract another group. Unless you want to be ultra-tidy, a few insect pests will not do much harm in a well-run garden, so do not reach for the spray gun straightaway, but let the birds sort out the problem. Only resort to insecticides if the situation looks like getting out of hand, which in reality does not often happen.

Bees love flowers filled with pollen and honey. Old-fashioned flowers are particularly full of these, whereas modern hybrids are often less so. Herbs are also good bee plants. Some people are frightened of bees, but they will do you no harm unless you trap them by sitting or stepping on them. There is nothing more idyllic than sitting listening to a contented hum coming from a flower-filled border on a summer day.

rustling in the undergrowth

The rustling of foliage can also be restful. It may take quite a strong wind to get some leaves moving sufficiently to make a sound, but bamboos and tall grasses will whisper in even a gentle breeze. They both make good background plants, and even though they start as relatively small plants in pots they will soon make good-sized clumps.

Below: The sound of water tinkling into a pool is very restful. A small feature, such as this, will fit into any garden.

Below, right: Wind can create restful sounds, either by rustling leaves, or by activating chimes or aeolian harps.

MAKING A WATERSPOUT

Waterspouts can be bought in kit form from garden centres and other specialist outlets. Most of the best kits come with full instructions for installing both the plumbing and the electricity for the pumps. Spouts work best when they are attached to a wall, but avoid using a house wall because the water may seep back in. If there is any question, waterproof the wall first. The pool at the base can consist of a conventional garden pool, made of rigid plastic and planted with aquatic plants. Alternatively, it can be a reservoir below ground, such as a large plastic container or a small dustbin, which will hold the water and the pump. There should be a heavy metal grid across the top, and this is covered in large pebbles, which hide the container and the grill. The water from the spout splashes onto the pebbles and disappears below ground, leaving no standing water, making it the ideal solution for gardens with small children. However, it is essential that the children cannot gain access to the reservoir or fall through the grill.

1

A pipe can be pulled up through the cavity of a wall or brought up on the outside of a single-skin wall.

2

This can then be attached to a submersible pump in a hidden reservoir at one end and the spout at the other.

Bamboos and grasses can be left in place throughout winter and will continue to play their tune. At this time of year dead leaves on beech (*Fagus sylvatica*) and hornbeam (*Carpinus betulus*) hedges, which remain on the plants all winter, will also make a pleasing noise as they rustle together.

water on the move

Perhaps one of the most soothing noises in the garden is that of trickling or running water, and water in one form or another can be incorporated into even the smallest garden. In the smallest it can be a waterspout, with water trickling or arching out from, say, a wall, into a small pond, which need not be any bigger than a bucket. If there are children around it can disappear between stones into a reservoir safely hidden below ground rather than into a potentially dangerous pond. Fountains, again ones that have no visible surface water if necessary, can also be easily constructed in a small garden. Waterspouts are especially useful for small gardens because they take up little space and yet can have a tremendous effect.

Fountains and spouts tinkle, but water running down a stream or over a waterfall makes quite a different sound. Waterfalls can easily be constructed in a small garden, but cascades and streams, even though they need a bit more space, are still within the realms of possibility.

wind music

There are a variety of ways in which the wind can be harnessed to produce a pleasing sound. Rustling sounds have already been mentioned, but there is also a more musical noise that can be produced by such devices as wind chimes and aeolian harps. No matter how delightful these may seem to be to you, don't forget that some people, especially your neighbours, may find that constant music from these becomes tedious or even irritating, so save them for special occasions.

SOOTHING SCENTS

After sight, the sense most used in the garden is the sense of smell. Nearly everybody enjoys a pleasant fragrance, and when it comes to choosing plants for the garden, why not choose those that have double value: attractive flowers or foliage, plus a good scent.

Remember that different plants are fragrant at different times of day. This is mainly dependent on the time the insects that pollinate them fly – most of the evening- and night-smelling plants, for example, are pollinated by moths. When you are buying plants it is worth remembering this timing, as it could be important. There is little point, for instance, in filling the garden with flowers whose scent is borne in the afternoon if you are only at home to enjoy your garden in the evening.

Scent can come from either the flower or the foliage and sometimes both. Flowers need a warm day before their fragrance is noticeable. Some snowdrops are heavily perfumed but unless you are near them on a bright winter's day you would never notice it. Chocolate cosmos (*Cosmos atrosanguineus*) smells of nothing in a cool summer, but on a warm day it produces the wonderful scent of chocolate.

Some flowers, such as honeysuckle, jasmine and daphne, will perfume the air far around, while others are more jealous of their scent and you have to get close to them. Strangely, some scented flowers cannot be appreciated by sticking your nose in them; they can only be smelled at a distance, once the scent has matured.

Many plants have scented foliage but few betray the fact until the leaves are brushed or lightly crushed. Some plants – rosemary (*Rosmarinus*) and lavender (*Lavandula*) are obvious examples – should be placed next to a path or patio where people walk so that as they brush past them their scent is released. It is also a pleasure to run your fingers through them just to release the smell. Many herbs fall into this category – mints (*Mentha*), thyme (*Thymus*) and lemon balm (*Melissa officinalis*) being but three. Thyme is tough enough to be walked on and can be planted in cracks in the paving so that its delicious scent is released as you step on it.

fragrance and the house

Climbers and wall shrubs that have fragrant flowers can be planted against walls near to windows that are often open. Anyone who has slept in a room with wisteria clambering around the windows will know the experience only too well. Roses, honeysuckle, jasmine and others have the same wonderful effect.

If you have space it is always worth growing a few fragrant plants for the house. Sweet peas (*Lathyrus odoratus*) are the obvious choice, although there are also many border plants that will last well when cut and placed in water. When eating outside a posy of fragrant flowers on the table is always a treat.

plants to avoid

Most sweetly scented plants have evolved to attract moths and other such insects, which, the plants hope, will pollinate the flowers. Some flowers, however, are pollinated by flies, which are usually attracted to carrion or rotting meat. These plants, therefore, often emit a foetid smell to attract these flies and should be avoided in the small garden, no matter how attractive the flower, or you may find you entertain alone. Possibly the worst offender is the dragon arum (*Dracunculus vulgaris*). Others, such as *Lilium pyrenaicum* and *Phuopsis stylosa*, have a distinctly foxy smell, which many people dislike.

FRAGRANT FLOWERS

Choisya ternata (Mexican orange blossom)
Convallaria majalis (lily-of-the-valley)
Cosmos atrosanguineus (chocolate cosmos)
Daphne tangutica
Dianthus 'Mrs Sinkins'
Erysimum cheiri (*Cheiranthus cheiri*; wallflower)
Philadelphus 'Sybille'
Rhododendron luteum
Rosa 'Ena Harkness'
Sarcococca hookeriana (Christmas box)

FRAGRANT FOLIAGE

Aloysia triphylla (lemon verbena)
Geranium macrorrhizum (cranesbill)
Laurus nobilis (sweet bay)
Lavandula angustifolia (lavender)
Mentha spicata (spearmint)
Myrica gale (bog myrtle)
Myrtus communis (common myrtle)
Rosmarinus officinalis (rosemary)
Salvia officinalis (common sage)
Santolina chamaecyparissus (cotton lavender)
Thymus serpyllum (creeping thyme)

Ideally, lavender should be planted close to a path so that its delightful fragrance is released as people brush past it.

SOFT LIGHTS

If you entertain in the garden in the evening, you are likely to require some form of lighting to illuminate not only your dining area, but paths and other parts of the garden. When subtly lit, gardens can have a magical quality that is quite different from their day-time appearance.

Below: Candles and night lights create a soft light, perfect for dining or relaxing areas, especially if you want a romantic atmosphere.

Opposite, below: Coloured bulbs can be effective for festive occasions but should not be overdone at other times as they can become garish.

As much thought should be given to lighting as to other aspects of garden design. Some people simply flood the area with a bright halogen light, but this is usually coarse and does little justice to the garden, as well as being uncomfortable for anybody eating or entertaining under such a glare.

Lighting should be subtle, but adequate for the task, and it should be localized so that it illuminates what needs illuminating and no more. The secret of good lighting is the interplay between light and shade. A soft pool of light on a table is only that because it is surrounded by darkness. A tree or shrub with a light shining into it takes on the appearance that it does only because of the way the shadows cast by the branches and the surrounding darkness highlight the shapes on which the light falls.

Think carefully about what you want to light, how much light you want to provide and how you are going to provide it.

flooding the garden

Floodlights have their place, especially in parking areas or as security lights, but they are generally too harsh for most purposes. If you use them make sure that they are pointing downwards so that they do not spill light into the garden or onto your neighbour's. It can be blinding to have to walk up a path with a halogen light glaring in your eyes. An automatic switch that allows them to come on when you enter an area saves not only a lot of energy but also irritation. Such devices are particularly useful for security lighting.

paths

Paths need adequate lighting so that you can see where you are going, but it should not be so bright that the glare blinds you. Generally, the best type of lamps are those that direct their light down onto the path. There is a wide range of designs to suit all styles of garden, including some that are solar powered and collect enough energy during the day to provide a soft light along a path at night. However, most of these stay on all the time, which can be annoying.

entertaining

When you are entertaining in the garden, soft lights are the best to help create the right atmosphere. If food is being prepared, such as on a barbecue, there should be sufficient light for you to see what you are doing and prevent accidents, but elsewhere the light level can be kept subtle. There is a wide choice of lamps specifically designed for outdoor use, ranging from standard lamps and table lamps to ones that can be hung from trees or other supports. Using dimmer switches gives you the additional flexibility of having brighter lights while food is being prepared and being able to lessen the brightness when festivities start.

old flames

Candles give off one of the most romantic and flattering of lights. Even on the stillest nights there is some breeze, which may either blow out the candle, make it

Special features can be illuminated. It is more effective to spotlight them rather than floodlight the whole area.

1
An electric cable should be buried at least 1m (3ft) deep to prevent it being accidentally dug up.

2
To prevent the cable from being damaged, it should be covered with a layer of roofing tiles.

3
A tape of yellow and black stripes should be laid along its length to warn that there is a live wire below it.

LAYING AN ELECTRIC CABLE

Installing electricity for lighting or pumps should be carried out only if you know what you are doing. If you have any doubts at all, employ a qualified electrician. All cables used in the garden should be well protected, both from the weather and accidental damage. They are best laid below ground. The trench should be at least 1m (3ft) deep to make sure that the cable is not accidentally dug up or punctured, and special armoured cable for outdoor use should be used. Lay an alkythene pipe in the trench with the cable passing through it. Electrical piping should be coloured black. Alternatively, lay the cable along the centre of the trench and cover it with a layer of roof tiles. For added protection, lay a strip of brightly coloured tape on top of the tiles before backfilling with earth.

burn quickly or blow hot wax everywhere. It is a good idea, therefore, to enclose it in a glass shade or lantern of some sort. Torches, on the other hand, look best when they are blown about by the wind. The light is not steady enough to eat by but is perfect for more general lighting along a path or around a patio.

fairy lights

Small, white fairy lights or Christmas lights create a sparkling atmosphere and can be used for background lighting along paths or around a patio or more specifically for illuminating a sitting or eating area. These add a touch of liveliness to the scene. Make sure that the lamps you buy are for outside use.

lighting the trees

At night when you are indoors, the garden has usually disappeared. One way to give it life at this time of day is to illuminate selected areas of trees, shrubs or other vegetation. The effect will be quite different from that produced by daylight. The light will now normally come from below rather than above, giving everything a slightly eerie, ghostly feeling. Water can be lit in the same way.

TASTE OF THE COUNTRY – VEGETABLES

In recent years, as gardens have got smaller the vegetable plot has disappeared. Now, increasing numbers of people are beginning to realize what they are missing: taste. Home-grown vegetables may not look as perfect as those produced under the sanitized eye of the supermarket, but they will undoubtedly taste better. This may have nothing at all to do with the skill of the grower, but it will definitely have something to do with the freshness.

The problem with a small garden is that there is never enough space to do half the things you want to. Areas such as lawns and patios are multi-purpose because they can be used for relaxation, entertainment, play and other activities, such as hanging out the washing. Vegetable plots can only be used for growing vegetables, and so they are given a low priority when it comes to the allocation of space. It is, however, possible to grow quite a lot of vegetables in a small space as long as they are tended and as long as you do not grow things like rows of potatoes, which take up a lot of space (grow a few in tubs for that unique taste of new potatoes). Use raised beds where the soil can be kept fertile and where you can plant close together. Blocks are better space savers than rows. As soon as one crop comes off, replace it with another.

mixing it

Many vegetable plants are decorative and can happily mix with flower borders. The red stems of ruby chard, the frilly leaves of carrots and the colourful flowers of runner beans would all be worthy as ornamental plants, irrespective of their culinary qualities. The only problem with this type of approach is that you get gaps in the border when you harvest the vegetables, but the flowering plants do not last for ever either.

one for the pot

A surprising number of vegetables can be grown in containers of one sort or another. The most elegant type of container is the terracotta pot, but for convenience many vegetables, especially tomatoes and runner beans, are grown in plastic bags containing specially formulated compost. Containers can be placed anywhere in the garden as long as they are not in shade – tomatoes, for example, can be grown against a warm wall. Plants in containers need to be watered at least once a day, and in hot, dry weather they will require it more frequently.

allotments

If you are keen on growing vegetables – and it has a lot to recommend it – it is usually possible to rent an allotment not too far from your home. These are plots of land, usually at inexpensive rents, from which it is possible to feed a small family with a wide range of vegetables. Water is usually available, and many have allotment associations, whereby everybody who has an allotment on the site clubs together to get seed and materials at a discount. There are usually a number of experienced gardeners around, and a tremendous amount can be learned from them about practical gardening.

RECOMMENDED VEGETABLES FOR A SMALL GARDEN

Beetroot
Carrots
Courgettes
French beans
Leeks
Lettuce
Parsley
Radishes
Runner beans
Shallots
Spinach
Swiss chard
Tomatoes

Although usually used for
flowering plants, hanging
baskets can also be used for
vegetables such as lettuce
and tumbling tomatoes.

A more conventional way
of growing vegetables in
containers is to use pots.
Most vegetables can be
grown in them.

Bottom left: A trough full
of ornamental cabbages
and nasturtiums (*Tropaeolum
majus*), whose leaves can
be used in salads.

Bottom right: Containers of
varying heights with various
vegetables illustrate the
potential of small spaces
for growing produce.

GROWING VEGETABLES IN CONTAINERS

Beans, tomatoes and peppers can be grown in growing bags – that is, plastic bags filled with a special compost mix. Lay the bag down, cut up to three squares out of it and plant the plants through these. For other vegetables choose a large container, preferably one that is 45cm (18in) or more across. Place this in a sunny position. Make sure there are drainage holes in the bottom and place a layer of small stones over these to aid drainage. Fill the container with compost (buy growing bags and empty the compost into the container). Plant or sow the vegetables. Water daily and give a liquid feed once a week as soon as the vegetables start to swell.

OBJECTS OF DESIRE – SCULPTURE, *OBJETS D'ART*, TOPIARY

There is something immensely satisfying about using attractive objects in a garden. Even a garden that is dominated by plants still benefits from the occasional piece of sculpture, urn or even simply an old gnarled tree stump. Such objects provide something on which the eye can rest. However it should not just be any old object – a dustbin or an abandoned, rusty old car would not have the same effect. There are innumerable possibilities, some expensive, but others less so or even available for free.

sculpture

Sculpture has found a welcome place in our gardens ever since it was first created, and manmade objects of this type fit well with those of nature. The sculpture can be of any style or period that you like, although the setting will undoubtedly influence your choice – ultra-modern pieces might not fit well into a romantic- or cottage-style garden, for example. Pieces can be specially made for the garden, either by yourself if you are skilled or by commissioning them. This is likely to be expensive, however, and there are plenty of off-the-peg pieces at reasonable prices that can be bought. The sculpture can be positioned in isolation, as a focal point, perhaps at the end of a path or lawn, or it can be integrated into the rest of the garden, perhaps peering out between bushes or mixed with a collection of pots. It may be used in conjunction with something else – as a fountain or waterspout, for example – and many pieces, especially smaller pieces of sculpture, look better if they are lifted off the ground on a plinth of some sort.

topiary

Topiary has also played an important function throughout the history of gardens. This is the art of training shrubs to form shapes of various types. They may simply be geometric, such as a ball or cone, or they can be representative, peacocks being favourite shapes. They can be bought ready created, but this is an expensive option and there is no reason why gardeners should not create their own. Box (*Buxus sempervirens*) and yew (*Taxus baccata*) are the best shrubs to use as their foliage grows tightly.

objets trouvés

There are a large number of 'objects' that can make an attractive addition to the garden, taking the place of more formal (and more expensive) sculpture. Old tree stumps that have been worn into wonderful shapes by the weather make excellent points of interest. They may be posed by themselves or they can act as a base for pots or even another object. Although it is important to exercise discretion, old pieces of rusted metal can look extremely attractive, especially if they are pieces that naturally have a place in the garden, such as old watering cans or old tools.

Architectural reclamation businesses are a very useful source of all manner of objects, including pieces of carved stone, curious ironwork and a host of other things. Old chimneys or pipes can make good containers for plants or be used as objects in their own right. A less expensive place to look is along the seashore, especially after a storm when all kinds of floating debris can be found, from curious shaped bits of wood to old buoys and floats.

Opposite: Sculpture is the perfect accompaniment for plants in a garden. If well positioned, it never looks out of place and enhances the scene.

Below: Small scale topiary can be grown in containers, which is perfect for the garden, both because of the scale and the fact that it can be moved.

1 Start your topiary art by clipping a plant (such as box) into the shape required.

2 It may take several seasons before the plant has filled out in all directions.

①

②

TRAINING TOPIARY

An existing bush can be 'carved' into a simple shape, but it will take several years to recover and completely conceal the exposed inner branches with leaves. In many ways it is better to start with a young bush and train it as it grows. Simple shapes can be achieved by cutting the branches as they reach the required length. For a ball, for example, all the stems should be cut at an equal distance from the centre. Making a wooden template as a guide makes sure that the shape is maintained when the shrub is clipped each year.

More complicated shapes need an armature inside them. This can be of metal or wood. The branches are tied to this as they grow and trimmed to the desired shape. The armature should be made before the shrub grows too large and will therefore show for a few years until growth is complete. At this point it should be hidden. It can be left in place to help maintain the shape or removed once the shrub is fully established.

PRIVATE SPACE

One of the problems of turning a small garden into an outdoor room is that, unlike an inside room, it is not enclosed. There is little privacy. There are neighbours just over the fence; neighbours looking out of their windows; neighbours making a noise and smells; and people and cars passing by and aircraft flying overhead. It can be a nightmare of prying, noise, smells and other pollution and not the relaxing oasis that you would like it to be. We are social animals, but we all like our privacy and as much outside as inside. Quite a lot can be done to overcome these and other problems.

It is vital to be able to turn your garden into your own private space, a place which you are able to relax and revive your energies. The first thing is to get rid of your neighbours and the easiest legal way is to hide them, building up your boundaries so that they simply vanish behind them. This may take time, but in the long run it will be well worth it. Once the boundaries begin to thicken up, the noise and smells begin to diminish – you will never get rid of them completely, but enough to make life tolerable and your garden more of a haven.

HIDEAWAYS

One way of making doubly sure that you can get away from the neighbours is to build yet another insulating layer around yourself. Hideaways, such as arbours, which are tucked away in the garden, will help to blot out the outside world and will also help to reduce interference from the inside world. An arbour will also allow you to get away from other members of the family or, indeed, to come together with them in intimate seclusion. Life is not all about hiding from others but there are times in this busy world when it helps.

EYESORES

There are often other things to hide besides your neighbours and yourself, such as objects that do not quite fit into the garden scene but cannot be readily disposed of. You may, for example, have an ugly garage or shed, or there may be an oil tank that stands out like a sore thumb. Most people have to find space for dustbins and other utilities, which are not the most beautiful of objects. If they can be hidden away in some way, perhaps behind an attractive trellis screen, life will be just that little bit more pleasant.

GOING PUBLIC

As always, there is also the reverse of the coin. Opening gardens to the public is becoming big business as a means of raising money for charities. If you are pleased with the design and general appearance of your garden and do not mind strangers tramping around it, it can be an enjoyable and satisfying way to raise some money for your favourite charity. The great majority of visitors are pleasant and no trouble to have round for one day a year. Some will come to be inquisitive but others will come in search of ideas, just as you might have done yourself when you were planning the layout of your garden. If you have room and energy to provide teas and a plant sale, even more cash can be raised.

PERSONAL SPACE

To be successful, any garden should be a personal one. It should reflect the interests, aspirations and the character of its owner. A naturally untidy person is likely to have an informal space while a stickler for neatness is more likely to have a formal one, or at least one with a very clear design.

By impressing their personality on the garden, the owner makes it into a very personal space: it is unique. They are not copying somebody else. In the first place it is a garden for the gardener to enjoy, but when others visit it, the uniqueness will stand out and visitors will be more interested and impressed with it than they would if it were but a copy of many other gardens.

While it is a good thing to plan and design a garden, let it evolve about you, so you get something that the end result is something that you really want.

HIDING THE NEIGHBOURS

Most of us like our private lives to be private and to feel that we can act in the garden in the same way, within reason, as we can in the privacy of our own home. There is little we can do, short of moving, that will totally obliterate our neighbours but it is possible to reduce their impact to within reasonable bounds.

MAKING A FEDGE

A fedge is a cross between a fence and a hedge. It takes up less space than hedge, is less greedy, and is easy to create and maintain. First, erect a wire fence using chain-link or wire-netting. Knock posts into the ground at 1.8m (6ft) intervals. Stretch a length of galvanized wire between the tops of the posts, another halfway down and a third just above the ground. Next attach the netting wiring to the main wires. Plant ivies at 60cm (2ft) intervals along the fence and allow them to scramble up over the wire. The ivy will eventually cover it completely, creating a narrow hedge. Trim it back once a year, in spring, as you would a normal hedge.

One obvious way of coping is to erect solid walls or fences, which will certainly help to keep out prying eyes, especially if they are about 2.1m (7ft) high. If a fence already exists, try to establish whose it is before you rip it down. If it is not yours you cannot expect your neighbour to replace it unless it is unsafe, and so you may have to erect another on your territory. This is not usually necessary with wooden fences, but if, for example, the existing fence is no more than a few strands of wire, a solid fence will serve your needs much better. If you do erect a fence against a neighbour's, do not use their posts as they will be entitled to remove them, which would leave you with a bit of a dilemma. It is always good thing consult with your neighbours, or at least advise them, when you erect fences, walls or hedges to prevent antagonism.

soft option

Using plants to create privacy is the gardener's solution to the problem. These plants may form a hedge, but they could equally be plants set further into your garden so that they form a thick barrier of foliage between areas where you sit or entertain and the boundary. Virtually any plants will suit the latter purpose, although shrubs make a more permanent feature. Tall grasses and herbaceous plants will make a screen in summer, but will be of little use in winter, when it might not matter anyway. The advantage of using herbaceous material is that it creates a constantly changing scene, unlike one that is composed entirely of shrubs.

Evergreens make a year-round barrier and are especially valuable next to noisy roads. Yew and holly are slow growing but eventually form a dense hedge, which will absorb sound as well as providing visual privacy.

doing it with climbers

Trellis with climbers over it is a good way of providing privacy as they tend not to be too dense and disappear in winter, when privacy in the garden is not as important as in the height of summer. The lack of tall, thick boundaries in winter will make both your and your neighbour's garden lighter during this gloomy time of year.

combat noise with noise

You should not fall into the habit of thinking that anything your neighbours can play you can play louder, but it is possible to drown noise locally by creating an alternative. For example, a tinkling waterspout or fountain close to where you are sitting will do a lot to displace more distant noises from a neighbouring garden. This will not drown out anyone who is determined to make a lot of noise but it will make life easier in more normal situations.

keeping a sense of proportion

Do not go to extremes and raise a 10m (30ft) high hedge of leylandii (x *Cupressocyparis leylandii*) or you may end up with court battles on your hands. There is no need to antagonize neighbours by making their garden unpleasant. Tall hedges not only cut out the light but are hungry and can make it impossible to garden anywhere near them. They can also overpower the house and make it dark.

A shady gazebo provides
a quiet retreat on a warm
summer day.

INTIMATE HIDEAWAYS

There is something pleasurable about having cell-like hideaways, even in a small garden, to which you can disappear, perhaps to sit and read, perhaps to snooze, or even, if it is big enough, to entertain. Intimate arbours and larger pergolas permit both of these. It is also possible to screen off one part of the garden from another by creating internal barriers of one sort or another.

SUNFLOWER BARRIER

In autumn or winter dig a 60cm (2ft) trench across the garden where you wish the barrier to be, adding to the bottom as much well-rotted organic material, such as garden compost, as you can. In early spring sow some sunflower (*Helianthus*) seeds in pots, allowing two seeds to each pot. Place them in a warm position out of direct sunlight. Once they have germinated, remove the weaker of the two seedlings if both have come up. As the roots fill the pot, move on to a larger size. Once the threat of frosts has passed – usually in late spring or early summer – plant out the sunflowers in two rows in the trench at intervals of 30–45cm (12–18in). They will rapidly grow into an attractive tall screen for summer and last well into autumn.

Arbours are one of the greatest inventions in gardening. They allow you to create a room that is enclosed and 'safe' and yet at the same time open to the air and to the elements. They also enable you to grow some of your favourite plants in close proximity, especially climbing ones, which are allowed to clamber over the structure.

The structure itself need not be anything more elaborate than a few poles firmly stuck in the ground, with crossbars to support the roof of vegetation. There are many elaborations on this, including incorporating trellising in three of the sides and on the roof to make it easier to attach the climbers.

An arbour should be big enough to accommodate at least a seat, but preferably a bench. If you want to entertain there, there should be enough room for a table and chairs and room to walk around them to serve. A summerhouse is a more solid version of the same thing.

pergolas

Pergolas are generally larger and lighter than arbours, and they are constructed over paths and walkways. The same principle can, however, be used for making dining areas. Again, the structure is based on posts with a 'roof' to support plants, but in this case the sides are much more open – a pergola is, in effect, a leafy roof supported on posts. Vines make excellent plants for growing over pergolas, which are perfect for filtering out the sun and also for providing a screen from neighbours who might be watching from their upstairs windows.

internal barriers

A garden that reveals everything in one glance can be rather boring. It is much better to break up the plot so that some areas remain hidden until you get to them. The barriers can be created from shrubs, arranged in vague lines or even used to make a formal hedge, although in a small garden an internal hedge can be a waste of space. Picket fences can be rather attractive, particularly if you have a cottage-style garden.

The best approach to creating internal barriers is probably to use some form of trellising. Rustic trellis is cheap and can look effective, especially when it is covered with roses. The trellis can be easily made from rough poles, but if you want a more formal appearance, use poles that have been turned to a smooth, regular finish. Another option is to buy ready-made trellis panels, which are available in various designs and sizes. Even when they are draped with climbers, none of these trellises will be totally covered, and they offer tantalizing glimpses of what is hidden beyond.

a clearing in the forest

A hideaway need not, of course, be as formally organized as any of the preceding. All that is required is that a relatively enclosed space is created. If you have room for plenty of shrubs and perhaps a small tree or two, a private space can be created simply by making a clearing in the thicket and perhaps paving it or creating a small lawn if it is not too overhung with trees.

Arbours surrounded by foliage
make a very intimate hideaway,
either just for sitting in or, if it
is large enough, for dining in.

CONCEALING EYESORES

Every small garden seems to have its eyesore, and there is a danger that you get so used to it that you no longer notice it, but it will spoil your efforts to create an attractive garden or outside space.

Anything that does not form part of the garden picture as you envisage it, particularly anything that is ugly, can be construed as being an eyesore. It may be something large, such as a garage or shed, or it could even be something small that, because it is in the wrong place, stands out, such as a drain cover. Oil tanks rarely look attractive. Sometimes the problem is not necessarily that it looks wrong but that it might be a danger and needs covering. Examples of this would be a greenhouse or cold frame, whose glass could present a danger to young children.

In most small gardens eyesores tend to stand out. Evasive action should be taken to hide or disguise them. If the garden is broken up with screens, shrubs, tall plants or some other device , such objects are less likely to be seen.

a lick of paint

One of the simplest ways of disguising something is to paint it. A green oil tank, for example, is not as noticeable as one in another colour. The same applies to garages and sheds. Another approach is do the opposite and paint the object in such a way that it becomes a feature. In a modern garden or one with lots of objects (as distinct from plants) in it, the oil tank could be painted in all kinds of ways, including covering it with naturalistic or abstract designs.

the art of disguise

The gardener's solution is to cover the offending item with plants. This can be achieved simply by letting plants scramble over a garage or shed or indirectly by placing a trellis in front of the offending object and allowing the plants to climb up this. Allowing plants to climb directly over a garage or shed can create a problem if you have to paint the wall regularly or treat a shed with preservative, because the climber will have to be removed. Ivy is one of the best covering plants because it has the advantage of being evergreen. To add interest in summer you can always plant one or two clematis to climb up through it. The viticella types are most suitable in these situations because they are cut the ground each spring and do not give the ivy the chance to smother them.

Erecting trellis in front of structures is a good way of protecting children from the dangers of falling into the glass in a greenhouse or cold frame. If necessary, place the trellis completely around the structure with a gate for adult access. As the children become older, the gate can be removed, allowing easier access.

coping with drain covers

When it comes to disguising annoying objects like drain covers and inspection hatches, the answer is quite simple: place a container of plants on it. There are plenty of trough-like containers that will conceal the entire cover, although you should bear in mind that if the cover ever needs to be opened the container should not be so heavy that it is impossible to move. An alternative is to position a group of smaller pots, which are easier to move, on the lid. If the cover is in a border, plant something like New Zealand burr (*Acaena* spp.), which will spread across the cover and disguise it but which can be easily cut back if you need to open the hatch. If you cover it in this way, make sure you have a record of where it is.

utility areas

Many gardens have areas that house utilitarian objects such as dustbins and washing lines, or perhaps are used to store bicycles or a cement mixer or just the odds and ends that most households seem to accumulate and that, although they do not use them, they are loathe to discard. A trellis screen may solve the problem, or a panelled fence can be used to hide the items completely. If this looks a bit stark, plants can be grown over or in front of it.

PLANTS FOR SCREENING

All the following are slow to start with, but some, especially the *Fallopia* (note its common name) and the *Parthenocissus*, are more vigorous and may be unsuitable for covering a small wall. The others will cover about the same area in about the same time, but the density of their leaves varies.

Clematis montana
Clematis viticella
Fallopia baldschuanica (mile-a-minute plant)
Hedera helix (common ivy)
Humulus lupulus 'Aureus' (golden hop)
Hydrangea anomala subsp. *petiolaris* (climbing hydrangea)
Lonicera periclymenum (common honeysuckle)
Parthenocissus henryana (Chinese Virginia creeper)
Rosa 'New Dawn'

COPING WITH CHILDREN

Children – our own, or other people's – may use the garden more than we do, and their needs must be taken into consideration and incorporated into any garden makeover. Any attempt to ignore them and create an immaculate lawn with perfect beds may come to naught once the children start to play.

The key to planning for children is to provide what they would like rather than what the adults would like. Children are often happy with the simplest of things, such as an open space to play on and a secret place in the bushes, which they can adapt for all kinds of real and imaginary games. Structures such as climbing frames and sandpits should be designed with the child in mind rather than being selected for what will look attractive or fit in with the garden

With some thinking ahead, however, the playthings that you provide for the children can be turned into something else once they have outgrown them. A sandpit, for example, can be transformed into a pond. A wooden climbing frame can be clad with timber and become a shed or a summerhouse. A playhouse might become a bicycle shed or a store of some sort. They can be originally sited and constructed with this potential conversion in mind.

security

In many respects the garden should be an ideal place for children to play, as it should be secure in terms both of keeping them within a defined space and in sight and also of determining what they play with. There should be gates at all access points, and the gates should be so constructed that young children can neither slip through the bars nor climb over the top. They should also have child-proof catches or locks on them.

poisonous plants

A problem – potentially a serious problem – that is often overlooked is checking to see if there are any dangerous plants in the garden. Some plant are poisonous and if eaten can cause vomiting or even death. Other plants exude sap that, if it is allowed to get onto the skin, can cause severe irritation. In the middle of children's play anything in the garden is likely to become part of some imaginary game, and food and feeding may be part of the game. Poisonous berries or shoots and leaves can be transformed into imaginary sweets or other foodstuffs. Do not risk it. Get rid of the plant. If it is something you particularly like, you can always replace it when the children have grown up.

they are never too young

Children love to imitate the adult world, and it is never to early to teach them about gardening. Although they will soon get bored helping their parents, they will spend longer on something if they are allowed to do their own thing. A small space allocated as a child's garden together with a few plants and packets of seed can work wonders. Choose seed that will germinate and produce shoots rapidly – radishes and marigolds are ideal – or they will quickly become bored with waiting. Don't get too exasperated if the 'garden' ends up just a mess of weeds; you can always try again the following year.

POISONOUS PLANTS

Aconitum spp. (aconite, monkshood)

Arum spp. (lords and ladies)

Brugmansia (*Datura*) spp. (Angel's trumpets)

Colchicum spp. (autumn crocus)

Daphne spp.

Digitalis spp. (foxglove)

Euphorbia spp. (spurge)

Heracleum mantegazzianum (giant hogweed)

Laburnum spp.

Ligustrum spp. (privet)

Rhamnus spp. (buckthorn)

Ruta spp. (rue)

Solanum spp.

Taxus spp. (yew)

Wisteria spp.

Left: Play areas for children should be visible from the house. Soft surfaces like chipped bark make for safe play.

Top right: Toys such as this windmill can add to the interest of the garden for adults as well as children.

Bottom right: Sand pits for children are always fun and are heavily used. Use washed river sand not builder's sand.

PLAY AREAS

Once the children take over in a small garden they are likely to take over the whole space. It may help to designate certain areas specifically for play, and an advantage of this is that you can use softer surfaces to prevent too may knocks and bruises. The challenge, of course, is to try to create something that the children will like.

CAMPS

Somewhat in the same vein as a playhouse, children love to build 'camps', and if part of the garden can be put aside for this it is likely to give hours of pleasure. An area tucked out of sight, possibly at the furthest point of the garden from the house, will be best, especially if it is hidden amid a thicket of shrubs. Not much space will be required and only a few shrubs are needed. If they already exist, large rhododendrons are ideal, because they have a 'ready-built' space below them. Let the children make their own camp, but it may be an idea to prune back some at least of the shrubs to create the space for them. These take several years to grow, so it may be worth thinking about creating this space well in advance so that it can be a proper feature. You may need to be prepared to replant the shrubs once the children have grown out of their space.

Axonopus (carpet grass) – warm climates
Eremochloa ophiuroides (centipede grass) – warm climates
Lolium perenne (perennial ryegrass) – cool climates
Paspalum notatum (bahia grass) – warm climates
Poa pratensis (Kentucky blue grass) – cool climates

The one thing that most children will want, often right up through adolescence, is a tough lawn on which they can play games. There is no point at all in trying to create a smooth, billiard-table lawn of soft grasses if your children want to play football and ride their bicycles.

soft landings

In areas where children climb or are likely to fall it is a good idea to cover the ground with bark chippings, which are relatively soft and will help cushion the fall. It is not the equivalent of a feather mattress, and anyone will be hurt if they fall from a height or fall awkwardly, but it will reduce the number of grazes and bruises. Rake it over occasionally and top it up so that there is a constant depth of no less that 5cm (2in).

climbing frames

Climbing frames can be made at home or bought for home assembly. Home-made frames will probably be made of wood. Make absolutely certain that they are sturdy, stable and unlikely to collapse. There should be no awkward corners or holes in which fingers can become trapped, and the wood should be smooth and splinter free. Ready-made ones may be of metal or wood. Follow closely the manufacturer's instructions for erection and make sure that they are securely fixed to the ground.

playhouses

Playhouses are fun for children. It is possible to buy a ready-made version, but it is probably more satisfying to make your own, especially if you plan into it some future use for when the children have grown out of playing with it. It can be to your own design or based on one of the children's favourite stories. Safety and stability are the priorities, no matter what the design.

A more adventurous adaptation of having a playhouse is to build a tree house. This is, obviously, more appropriate for older children, but adults often get as much fun out of it as their children do. It can really be built in a tree if there is one, but it can equally well be above ground in some other way, such as being built on sturdy stilts of lengths of redundant telegraph poles. It can be a fine work of architecture or it can be left up to the children, when it is more likely to resemble a disreputable shack. Before you build a tree house, check the planning regulations in your area to make sure that you do not need planning permission.

sandpits

Sandpits never seem to be out of favour with children. Generation after generation, children spend hours building castles and knocking them down. With forethought, a sandpit can be constructed in such a way that it is turned into a garden pond once the children have grown up. If the pit is constantly supervised then it is possible to have a combined sandpit and paddling pool.

Top left: Children should be kept away from water. They seem to have a natural instinct to play with it, but accidents can happen.

Bottom left: One way of having a water feature that is safe for children is to fill the pool with large pebbles so that there is no standing water.

Right: For older children, tree houses have tremendous appeal. They must, however, be safe, and in some areas, you may need planning permission.

HELPING WILDLIFE

Many people enjoy gardening because they feel it brings them a little closer to nature. This may be a cliché, but it is true that working in a garden makes you aware not just of the soil in your hands and what lives in it but also of the birds, insects and animals around you. You become more conscious of what they look like and of the way they live. There is nothing more delightful than weeding near a pond as colourful dragonflies glide past.

The multiple pressures on the countryside from housing and roads mean that any extra help that can be provided to both the plant and animal communities is most welcome. Providing food and habitats for birds and other animals and allowing wildflowers into the garden creates a reservoir that may eventually be used to replenish other areas as they become available. Every little helps in the fight to preserve the countryside, even if your garden is in the centre of a town.

One of the great advantages of looking after nature is that it will help you look after your garden. If you grow a wide range of flowering plants, especially some of the old-fashioned ones, these will attract hoverflies, lacewings and ladybirds to your garden. These insects will, in turn, help you control pests such as greenfly. Encourage birds and animals to come into the garden, and they will help rid you of various pests. Tits and dunnocks, for example, will eat greenfly, and thrushes, hedgehogs and toads will help to keep the snail and slug population under control. Greenfly and slugs are two of the worst pests in the garden, and anything you can do to encourage nature to help you to control them will make your life much easier.

SHEER PLEASURE

There is something enormously enjoyable and rewarding about being part of nature and being surrounded by butterflies and birds as you work or relax in the garden. There is a world of difference between sitting on a barren, undecorated terrace with your eyes shut and with only the noise of neighbours in your ears and sitting near a herb garden, listening to the drowsy hum of bees and watching butterflies flit from flower to flower.

There is much you can do when you plan your garden makeover to encourage different forms of wildlife to inhabit or visit your garden. You can provide them with food and drink, and with places to perch and roost as well as boxes in which to nest and bring up the next generation. Parts of the garden can be given over to growing wildflowers, partly for their own preservation and partly as food for birds and insects, which generally prefer native plants to introduced ones.

PASSING IT ON

A love of nature is an undying passion, which can be practised anywhere. It is a pleasure that is well worth passing on to children, who will be more inclined to follow in your footsteps if they are surrounded by the sight and sound of birds and insects as well as wildflowers. It will become part of their lives if they are allowed to experience it at first hand, and they are likely to continue with their fascination long after their childhood.

A wildlife refuge in a town will never replace the real countryside but it will certainly help to preserve many of the plants and creatures that the town has squeezed out. The range of animals that will be attracted to a natural garden is surprising. It is a good idea to keep notes of birds and other animals you see and over the years you will build up a fascinating record. Although you will introduce most of the plants yourself, quite a number will arrive in the form of seed blown in from elsewhere or brought in on the soil of another plant. They even may drop from an animal's coat or feet. Again, keep records and your fascination will grow.

FEEDING BIRDS

Birds spend an inordinate amount of time feeding, either just themselves or providing for their young. A small garden can provide the right kind of environment where there is plenty of food for them, and they will be inclined to return regularly rather than going off to search for a new source of supply. Feeding not only means putting out peanuts, to which only a limited number of birds will be attracted, but providing plants in the garden that will produce a natural supply of food.

The simplest way to provide food for birds is, of course, to buy peanuts and wild bird seed and put them out. When you are designing your garden it is worth thinking about where such things as bird tables should go. This is not so much of a problem for free-standing ones, but if you want to have a table that is suspended somewhere, more thought must go into it. From the birds' point of view, it does not much matter where it is as long as it is safe from surprise attacks from cats. On the other hand, many people derive great pleasure from watching birds eat, and so you should consider placing the bird table so that it can be seen from a window, preferably from where you do mundane things such as washing up to help relieve the tedium.

feeding in style

The style and decoration of the feeders is of little consequence to the birds, but they should be of a type that can easily be dismantled and cleaned. Cleaning may be a chore, but it is essential for the health and well-being of the birds. The only other aspect of design that may be worth considering is to choose a feeder that allows the smaller birds to get their fill as well as the larger, generally rather bullying ones. In some areas squirrels can be a problem, too. Nuts, grains and fat represent good sources of food. They can be provided separately or bound together by melting the fat and pouring it over the other ingredients.

natural food

Berries and seeds represent the major part of many birds' diets, and these can be provided by including the trees, shrubs and other plants that bear them in your garden layout. Some of the smaller trees are ideal for birds. For example, many of the mountain ash or rowans (*Sorbus* spp.) and holly (*Ilex aquifolium*) provide berries, and birch (*Betula* spp.) produces plenty of seed. There are several bushes that bear berries, some of which are gobbled up quickly while others are left until times of shortage.

Perennial plants are also a useful supply of foodstuffs in the form of seeds. Goldfinches and many other birds will come in large numbers to feed on seedheads that have been left on. Leaving old vegetation standing throughout the winter can make a garden look rather unkempt and untidy, but it is worth leaving at least some throughout winter. This old vegetation is also a hiding place for many insects, and insect-eating birds will also come seeking food.

on the ground

Blackbirds and many other birds like to scrabble through the old leaves on the ground. Although fallen leaves should be cleared away from lawns and other areas such as steps, where they may become slippery and be dangerous, if possible allow some to remain under the hedgerows for the birds to explore. In cold weather these are the last places to freeze, and they often provide the birds with vital supplies of insects, grubs and seeds.

TREES AND SHRUBS FOR BERRIES

Berberis thunbergii (barberry)
Cotoneaster horizontalis
Crataegus monogyna (quickthorn, hawthorn)
Daphne tangutica
Ilex aquifolium (common holly)
Ligustrum lucidum (Chinese privet)
Rosa glauca (rose)
Sorbus hupehensis (Hubei rowan)
Symphoricarpus albus (snowberry)
Viburnum opulus (guelder rose)

Bird feeders are one of the simplest methods of attracting birds to the garden and they will give pleasure out of all proportion to their cost.

1
A simple bird table can be constructed from a flat piece of wood and four thin pieces of rope.

2
Hang it from a branch where it can be seen and preferably where cats cannot get at it. Clean it regularly.

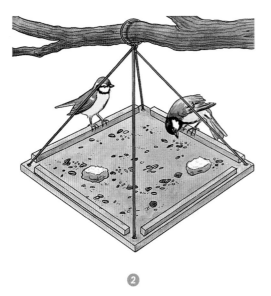

A SIMPLE FEEDER

A basic bird feeder can be constructed from a square or rectangle of wood about 25–30cm (10–12in) across. Drill a hole in each corner and attach a string through each one. Tie the strings to a ring so that the wood is kept horizontal and hang it from a branch of a tree. To prevent food falling off, a narrow piece of wood can be attached along each edge, but do not allow the edging pieces to meet in the corners – if you leave a small gap in each corner, rainwater can drain away freely and it will be easier for you to clean up any uneaten food.

OFFERING A HOME – NEST BOXES, SHRUB COVER, WALL CLIMBERS

In addition to offering birds food, another way to attract and help them is to provide shelter for them, which may be for roosting, for protection in inclement weather or for nesting in. The shelters will either be in trees or shrubs or against or in buildings. It is difficult, and undesirable, to force birds to go anywhere unless they want to, so the key to success is to provide as large a selection of sites as possible.

It is not always possible to say what makes a desirable residence for a bird, although several factors seem obvious. The first is security. They like somewhere they are likely to be free from attack, which generally means somewhere they cannot easily be seen. Being hidden from sight normally means that there is also some protection from the weather, although this does not appear to be top priority.

Another important fact is that there should be somewhere to support the nest. A fork in a hedge that has enough branches to support the structure but not too many to make access difficult seems to be the general requirement. Hedges that are relatively compact but that do not have too tight a mesh of branches appear to be the ideal. Open trees are favoured only by large birds such as magpies and crows.

It is difficult to predict where birds will choose to nest, and all that the gardener can do is to provide them with plenty of opportunities. Close, dense bushes are better than open ones.

home-made comforts

Nest boxes are often a sure way of attracting nesting birds, especially as the number of old trees with holes in them seems to be on the decline because they are often deemed dangerous and cut down, especially in urban areas. The birds are not fussy about the shape or outward appearance of the box: they just want shelter and security. The one thing they are fussy about is the entrance hole, with different birds preferring different sizes, As a rule, they tend to prefer nesting in boxes with holes they can just squeeze through. The material is unimportant to the birds, although gardeners are more likely to prefer wood to plastic. Make a box about 15cm (6in) square and 20cm (8in) tall with a round hole, about 2.5cm (1in) in diameter, in one side and a slanting, removable lid. Attach the box to a tree with wires around the trunk.

Nest boxes should be sited in a secure position away from predators, especially cats and children. They should also be placed so that they are not in direct sunlight, or the young birds will die of excessive heat. It is also a good idea to position the entrance hole away from the prevailing winds so that rain is not blown in.

Informal nest boxes, such as large tin cans, stuck on their side in the middle of a hedge are often successful and will frequently be used by birds for shelter as well as for nesting.

shelter

If it is difficult to predict where birds will nest, it is equally difficult to tell where they will roost. In their quest for security and shelter, birds often find a place out of sight and out of the wind and rain. Although their feathers keep them warm and dry, most birds seem to prefer to get out of the weather if it is unpleasant. Again, provide as many types of shrub as you have room for. Hedges are still one of their favourites, although they will often hide inside open-sided buildings if there are perching places available.

Climbing plants often offer homes to many types of birds. Clinging to the side of a building, such sites are stable, and the wall often provides a certain amount of warmth. They also offer protection from predators.

Opposite: Nest boxes are always fascinating to watch when they are in use. Site them in an area where the birds will not be interrupted.

WILDFLOWER GARDENING

When you are thinking about making over you garden it is worth considering whether you should replace some of your conventional flowerbeds with those containing native wildflowers. Although they are not as flamboyant as the highly bred border plants, many are attractive in a quiet way. They also have the advantage of attracting birds, butterflies and beneficial insects to the garden.

The best way to grow wildflowers is in a meadow setting. The scale of a small garden makes this difficult, but there is no reason why you should not devote a border to wildflowers or why, if you have no need of it, you should not turn part or all of your lawn into a wildflower reserve.

making a meadow

The one thing that you do not want in your meadow is coarse grasses, which will swamp the flowers. Starting from a lawn is ideal because most of the grasses there are soft, making a perfect background for the wildflowers. It is not easy to sow flower seed into a lawn, and you will have much better results if you buy or grow the plants in pots and transfer them in a random pattern to the lawn. Once established, they will soon self-sow to produce more plants.

If you are starting with a bare patch of ground, remove all weeds, particularly the coarse grasses, such as couch, from the plot and sow a mixture of grass seed and wildflower seed. Alternatively, you can first sow a lawn and then plant into it.

The grass should not be cut in the meadow until the flowers have seeded, which will be in mid- to late summer. Cut the grass then and again in autumn so that it is reasonably short for the winter.

odd places

Most gardens have a few odd corners that are not formally organized into a garden. These often make perfect spots to plant a few wildflowers. In the wild, hedgerows are often full of flowers, and the base of a hedge can be used as a wildflower refuge in the garden. This is also a good place to grow plants, such as woodlanders, which like a little shade.

You may not have the space or the inclination to turn over a whole area or border to wildflowers, but there is no reason why you should not grow a few in one of the general flower borders. Quite a number of native plants are bold enough to hold their own in a mixed border. Indeed, many of the plants we now grow have been derived from these wildflowers, and it makes a welcome change to revert to the simpler forms of their wild ancestors.

obtaining plants

You must never go out and dig up the plants you want from the countryside. Plants already growing in the wild should be left where they are, and many are, in fact, protected by law. Always buy your plants from a nursery, which are increasingly carrying wildflowers as part of their stock, or from friends who have raised the plants. You can also raise them from seed, which can easily be bought from seed merchants that specialize in wildflowers. Get children involved in sowing and growing the plants so that they acquire a lifetime's interest in wildflowers.

When you are choosing the plants to grow, look out for those that naturally grow in your area. Avoid the temptation to grow more exotic plants from elsewhere or to select the rarer ones. The latter are difficult to grow – that is usually why they are rare – and often need specialized conditions. Many seed merchants will make a up a seed mix to suit the area in which you live, providing an ideal starter pack.

A profusion of brightly
coloured wildflowers evokes
a sense of the countryside
in a small garden.

ATTRACTING BEES
AND BUTTERFLIES

Although most people seem to welcome butterflies to their gardens, they are equivocal about moths and even down-right hostile to bees, perhaps because they confuse them with wasps.

KEEPING BEES

Keeping bees is a fascinating occupation and one that provides a great deal of benefit to surrounding gardens. Bees are needed for the pollination of much fruit, for example, as well as lots of flowering plants. Bees are often kept in small gardens, and in towns this can be an invaluable service. However not everybody likes to have a beehive in the garden, and in a small garden it is difficult to get away from it, so unless the whole family is happy with the idea, don't do it. Locate the hive or hives away from the house and orientate it so that the main flight path is across your own garden and not that of a neighbour. If there are bushes not too far away from the hive, the bees will be forced up into the air so that by the time they leave your garden, no one will notice that there is a concentration of them. Always be prepared to go and collect swarms from neighbouring houses should the need arise. If one bee can be terrifying to someone, you can imagine what a whole swarm is like.

FLOWERS TO ATTRACT BEES AND BUTTERFLIES

Ageratum houstonianum (floss flower)
Aster novae-angliae (New England aster)
Buddleja davidii (buddleia)
Hedera helix (common ivy)
Lavandula angustifolia (lavender)
Limnanthes douglasii (poached egg plant)
Mentha spicata (spearmint)
Nepeta x faassenii (catmint)
Sedum telephium (orpine)
Thymus serpyllum (creeping thyme)

butterflies

It is hardly surprising that people like to see dainty butterflies flitting from flower to flower around the garden. They are the perfect complement to so many flowers, and there is no doubt that a great deal of pleasure can be derived from having butterflies in the small garden. They are the most delightful creatures, whose erratic flight does not seem to be at all threatening. Moths are often equally interesting but their more direct approach somehow often seems more ominous. Night-flying moths in particular often bump into people, which can be quite frightening. However, if you can overcome your fears, looking out for moths can be as rewarding, if not more so, than looking for butterflies, as there are many to discover, unlike butterflies of which there are only a handful of species.

One way to attract butterflies is to make sure that you have the types of plant that they like. Many of the flamboyant modern hybrids are sterile and are of little use for attracting wildlife, but most of the old-fashioned plants are full of nectar and are attractive to them. Plant these in a warm area and try to have a few butterfly plants in flower throughout spring, summer and autumn.

Wet summers and cold summers are disappointing for butterfly watchers, but there is little you can do about this. One thing you can do to help is to grow a few plants that butterflies breed on to make sure that there are adequate supplies for the following year. The problem is that most gardeners regard these plants as weeds and are unlikely to relish giving up part of their limited space to them. Stinging nettles, for example, are the breeding plant for the magnificent peacock butterfly, and if you can find an odd corner, tucked away behind a shed, for example, where you can leave a few nettles undisturbed, you will be doing a great deal for nature conservation.

bees

Although most of us love to hear bees droning away in the background, many people are rather frightened of them and would rather not have them at close quarters. In fact, unless they are attacked or frightened, bees do not pose a threat to anyone. It is often imagined that you need a large garden to keep bees, but in fact they are often kept in comparatively small gardens, even in roof gardens in the centre of towns and cities. Even if you do not keep bees yourself it is worth having plants they like in the garden, partly for the vital role they play in pollination and partly for their company.

Bees are attracted to a wider range of plants than butterflies, but old-fashioned plants again seem to be the most beneficial. Often it is the less conspicuous plants that are best loved. The herb garden, for example, is nearly always completely alive with butterflies, and yet herbs are far from the most flamboyant of plants and are often quite dull from the flowering point of view.

The hum of bees on a hot day creates a drowsy atmosphere which transports the gardener away to the middle of the countryside.

SOMEWHERE TO DRINK

Birds and animals need to drink as well as to eat, and so they need access to water. Birds also like water to wash in, as anyone who has watched a blackbird enjoying a bath will know. Another way of attracting wildlife to the small garden is, therefore, to provide water of some description.

Often within minutes of a pond being first filled wildlife will appear as if from nowhere to use it. Some will come just to drink, but others will come to live. Where they come from is difficult to tell, but water boatman will soon be skating over the surface, and water slugs, newts and frogs can be seen swimming in the water. Ducks may even fly in, and herons will come looking for fish, often soon after dawn, before there is anyone around to see them. Dragonflies will appear and will soon be laying their eggs.

Occasionally fish will appear without being introduced. No one is quite sure how this happens – some say the eggs are carried on the feet of ducks – but they will usually have to be introduced if you want them. Not all gardeners like to have fish in their ponds because they tend to eat a lot of the other pondlife, or at least the eggs and larvae, so reducing the water population. If you do want fish, choose the native varieties that need conserving – as does so much other wildlife. This is particularly true if you have a natural pond, in which goldfish and koi carp can look out of place.

During cold winters the water may freeze, and will not be available for those creatures that need to drink it. Freezing weather can also mean that life in the pond, below the covering ice, may be suffering, not so much from cold as from the lack of oxygen, which may be used up. In these circumstances, poisonous gasses accumulate under the ice. Tip ice off birdbaths and other receptacles and replace the water at frequent intervals. Do not break the ice on the pond because the shock waves can injure or kill fish. Place a bowl of hot water or some other hot object on the surface of the ice and melt a hole in it. You can buy special electric heaters, which can be inserted in the water and will keep part of the pond free from ice.

The pressure of ice can damage the structure of the pond itself. One way to reduce the chances of this is to float a ball or a piece of polystyrene on the surface to absorb much of this pressure.

birds

Birds will drink from a pond but they do not need a great deal of water – a small birdbath or dish of water will be quite sufficient. Unfortunately, small quantities like this quickly get polluted or dry out, so replace and replenish it at frequent intervals. Position the water not only where you have the pleasure of being able to watch but also where there is plenty of space around it so that the birds can see any approaching cats or foxes.

Deep ponds, with steep sides, are of no use to birds – apart from ducks – because they have no way of getting to the water's surface. Gently sloping sides allow much better access. Alternatively, float a piece of wood on the water on which they can perch.

animals

Many animals like to drink from ponds and, like birds, they may well find access difficult. If sloping sides are not possible, lay a length of wood from the shore into the water. This will not only allow access but also give any animals, such as hedgehogs, which fall into the water help with climbing out again. Drowning is a real threat in most garden ponds.

MARGINAL WATER PLANTS
Astilbe x *arendsii*
Caltha palustris (marsh marigold)
Hosta crispula (plantain lily)
Houttuynia cordata
Iris laevigata
Lobelia 'Queen Victoria'
Mimulus luteus (monkey musk)
Myosotis scorpioides (water forget-me-not)
Primula japonica (Japanese primrose)
Ranunculus lingua (greater spearwort)

A birdbath is not only an ideal place for birds to drink and bathe, but is also a point of sculptural interest in the garden.

A shallow pool with stones in it dug into a lawn makes the perfect drinking and bathing place for birds.

A SIMPLE DRINKER

Neither birds nor animals are particularly fussy about the decor of their drinking place – all they want is the water – so it possible to use the most basic of articles. An old dustbin lid, for example, let into a hole dug in the lawn and filled with water makes an ideal watering and bathing place for all kinds of wildlife. Such a lid is ideal because it is not too deep and the sides slope gradually, allowing any creature that falls in to find its way out. Wash and clean it out at regular intervals, preferably once a day, but at least once a week, to prevent the build-up of parasites and dirty water.

Page numbers in *italics* refer to illustrations

ACKNOWLEDGEMENTS

Front cover: OCTOPUS PUBLISHING GROUP LTD/Gareth Sambridge.

EDIFICE/Cole 58/Darley 113 right/Lewis 105, 119.
ELIZABETH WHITING ASSOCIATES 14, 20, 25, 42, 85, 91, 102, 108.
GARDEN EXPOSURES/Andrea Jones 24, 46 Top, 59, 70, 95/Derek Harris 46 Bottom.
GARDEN PICTURE LIBRARY/Christi Carter 99 right/Eric Crichton 10/John Glover 26, 45, 55, 57/Lamontagne 79/Howard Rice 78/Ros Wickham 84/Steven Wooster 12.
JOHN GLOVER 87, 99 left/Design: Alan Titchmarsh 111 left/Design: Julie Toll 121/ Design:Jonathan Baillie 107.
OCTOPUS PUBLISHING GROUP LTD/James Merrell 74/Gareth Sambridge 1/ Mark Winwood 4, 6 left, 6 right, 8, 12, 16, 18, 22, 31, 33 left, 34, 35, 38 left, 41 right, 41 Top Left, 61, 63, 64, 67 left, 68, 69, 73, 76, 77, 81, 83, 88, 89, 92 left, 92 Right, 96, 97 Bottom, 111 Top Right, 114, 117, 123, 125/Hilary Moore 86.
ROBERT HARDING PICTURE LIBRARY/L. Bond 113 Bottom Left.
HARPUR GARDEN LIBRARY/Jerry Harpur 10, /Design: Simon Fraser 18,/ Jerry Harpur/Design:Sonny Garcia, San Francisco 20/Marcus Harper/Design: Michael Balston for Daily Telegraph 39 right/Marcus Harpur/Design: Jonathan Baillie 48,/
Design:Barbara Thomas 51/Jerry Harpur 52.
ANDREW LAWSON 62, 113 Top Left/Margot Knox 28.
CLIVE NICHOLS PHOTOGRAPHY/Design:Joan Murdy 16/Designer: Ann Frith 27/ Robin Green/Ralph Cade 33 right/The Nichols Garden, Reading 97 Top, 111 Bottom Right.
MICHAEL PAUL 22.
DEREK ST ROMAINE/Christopher Costin, Hampton Court 1995 41 Bottom Left
MARK WINWOOD 6 Centre, 14, 36.